RUTKA'S
NOTEBOOK
A VOICE FROM THE HOLOCAUST

RUTKA'S
NOTEBOOK
A VOICE FROM THE HOLOCAUST

Before the Nightmare A view of Bedzin, Poland, Rutka Laskier's home, early in the 20th century. Towering over the Czarna Przemsza river are, at left, the town's castle, built in the 14th century, and, at right, the twin spires of the Jewish synagogue, which was burned to the ground soon after German troops entered the town in September 1939.

ISBN 10: 1-60320-019-3
ISBN 13: 978-1-60320-019-6
Library of Congress Number: 2008900481

Table of Contents

A Voice from the Holocaust

The Holocaust is a crime of such enormity as to defy comprehension. The details of Adolf Hitler's "Final Solution"—the systematic, factory-style murder of millions of human beings—are so hideous that we can be tempted to turn our eyes away from them. Too often we reduce this enormous tragedy to a single statistic: 6 million lives. And once thus quantified and diminished, it is all too easy to regard the Holocaust as an anomaly of history rather than an essential lesson of the wages of fanaticism, one that must never be forgotten.

Yet now and then a new story emerges from the war years, a story so compelling and so rooted in the details of daily life that it reminds us that the mass murder that is the Holocaust is a series of millions of individual crimes. The diary of Holland's Anne Frank opens a revealing window into the plight of those trapped in the horrors of the Third Reich, as does the story of Germany's Oskar Schindler. Recently the diary of a 14-year-old Polish girl, Rutka Laskier, has joined them, inviting us to view those stern days with new eyes.

That the diary was preserved is itself a minor miracle. Rutka Laskier was a bright Jewish girl whose well-to-do family lived in the middle-sized town of Bedzin in the area of southern Poland called Zaglembie. (The town's name is pronounced to rhyme with "engine" in English.) In 1939 almost half of Bedzin's 55,000 citizens were Jews; their ancestors had lived in the region since the Middle Ages. When Rutka's diary begins, it is early 1943, more than three years after the Germans conquered Poland. As her notebook entries show, Rutka and her friends knew that the Germans had now moved beyond harassing and demeaning Jews and were deporting them in massive numbers to "extermination" camps—where some 2 million Polish Jews had already died. Those who remained alive were beginning to realize what in fact was the case: such camps, in some of which Jews once labored as slaves, were now death camps where men, women and children were being killed en masse.

"The rope around us is getting tighter and tighter," Rutka writes. Hoping to preserve her diary for posterity, she made a pact with an older, non-Jewish friend, Stanislawa Sapinska: Rutka would conceal her diary in her apartment building when the Laskier family was moved to Kamionka, a shabby district on the outskirts of town where the Germans were relocating the city's Jews. When that day came, in late April 1943, Rutka hid the notebook, and when Sapinska returned to the apartment after the war ended, in 1945, she found it, in good condition.

Sapinska kept the notebook to herself for some 60 years, until she was persuaded to reveal its existence to the world. When the diary was published, first in Poland and then by Yad Vashem, Israel's Holocaust Remembrance Authority, it was hailed as a revelation. Now, TIME Magazine and Yad Vashem have joined hands to publish the first U.S. edition of this compelling historical document.

Diarist Rutka Laskier, 14, was aware as she wrote of the chilling fate that awaited her.

In this volume, the notebook is introduced by Zavaha (Laskier) Scherz, who tells the moving story of how she first learned of the existence of her murdered half-sister Rutka and then, decades later, of the diary Rutka had written. The text of the notebook is followed by Scherz's biography of her father, Yaacov, and by articles by Yad Vashem scholars that locate Rutka's tale within the context of her place and times. The editors have provided annotations and photographs to help convey the feel of life in occupied Bedzin in 1943.

In the pages of this book, Rutka's words reach out to us, across the span of more than 60 years, as she hoped they would. "Something in me has broken," she tells us. "I want to pour out on paper all the turmoil I am feeling inside," she tells us. "I'm turning into an animal waiting to die," she tells us.

This is no mere statistic: it is a human voice from which we cannot, we must not, turn away. Thanks to Rutka Laskier and Stanislawa Sapinska, we have been given a powerful new lens through which we can confront the horrors of the "Final Solution" and the evils that spring from racial and political fanaticism. Surely the appropriate response to this young, brave voice from the Holocaust is to listen, to remember and to bear witness. —*The Editors* ❖

The Sister I Never Knew

By Zahava (Laskier) Scherz

I was 14 years old when I came across the red photo album, hidden behind the arranged and starched bed sheets in my parents' home in Givatayim, outside Tel Aviv in Israel. The photos were from there, from the Holocaust. They were photos of my father Yaacov Laskier's family, all of whom had been exterminated in the Holocaust. All I had known was that before the war he had had four brothers, four sisters and his parents—and that was it.

In the album, there was a photo of a girl embracing a little boy. The girl was about 8 years old, with beautiful black, smooth hair. With a heavy heart, I turned to my father and asked him who those children were, and who was the girl who resembled me so much. And then, for the first time, my father told me about Rutka and Joachim-Henius, his children with his first wife, Dvorah (or Dorka) Hampel, born in 1904 in Bedzin, each of whom had perished in the Holocaust. Rutka was 14 years old when she died, exactly my age when I found out about her existence, and Henius was 6 years old. That is how I found out about my father's deceased children, and about his first life.

Fourteen years later, on September 24, 1977, in the early morning, a baby girl was born to my husband Avigdor and me at Hadassah Hospital on Mount Scopus, in Jerusalem—a sister to our son Yishai. We decided to call her Ruth, in honor of Rutka, which is Ruth in Polish.

Twenty-eight years later, on a Friday morning in January 2006, I received a phone call from Menachem Lior, a man I had never heard of. Lior presented himself as a Bedzin native who had emigrated to Israel after World War II and asked if I was Yaacov Laskier's daughter. When I acknowledged that I was, he became emotional and told me that a young girl's diary written during the Holocaust and hidden for 60 years had been recently found in Bedzin: the diary of Rutka Laskier. That morning, I started to get to know my sister Rutka—a very talented and beautiful girl, who, while being aware that she would not survive, wanted to document those days, in hopes future readers could follow her life and understand her death.

vi

Visions from the Past Rutka and Henius Laskier, 1938, from the prewar family album.

What had happened to her diary until its discovery in 2006? I learned about this in the year that followed, through a number of investigations and interesting worldwide encounters—some of them quite dreamlike. Among those I met were Stanislawa Sapinska, an 82-year-old Polish woman from Bedzin, the friend who had hidden Rutka's diary and then revealed it; Linka Gold, Rutka's onetime classmate, who lives in London; Adam Szydlowski, a journalist from Bedzin, who researches prewar Jewish life in Bedzin; and Bedzin survivors who live in Israel and who knew Rutka and others in the Laskier family.

Zahava (Laskier) Scherz, Ph.D., is Rutka Laskier's half-sister. A member of the faculty at the Weizmann Institute of Science in Rehovot, Israel, she also teaches at the Davidson Institute of Science Education in Rehovot.

I

This is the diary's story. Rutka, an exceptionally intelligent girl with fine writing skills, documented her life in her notebook during a few months of 1943. At that time, the Laskier family—Yaacov, Dvorah, Rutka, Henius and grandma Golda—were living in one room on the Kasernerstrasse, No. 13, in the open Jewish ghetto of Bedzin. The apartment belonged to Stanislawa Sapinska's family, and it was seized by the Germans when they established the Bedzin ghetto.

Stanislawa, then 20 years old, worked near the ghetto and used to visit the apartment from time to time at her father's request, in order to check on its condition. That is how she met Rutka, who, according to Stanislawa, was a serious, mature young girl, and they became friends. Stanislawa used to visit Rutka during her lunch break, and the two had many heart-to-heart talks. During my visit with Stanislawa, she told me that Rutka was well informed of the course of the war and the status of the military forces, as well of the fate of the deported Jews. Did Rutka have any contact with the anti-German underground? Stanislawa thinks she did.

During one of their encounters, Rutka told Stanislawa that she was writing a diary, and that she knew she would not survive the war. However, she wanted the diary to survive. The two girls decided that when the day came, Rutka would hide the diary underneath the double flooring of the staircase where she lived, and Stanislawa would take it and look after it.

In April 1943, the Laskier family left the house on the Kasernerstrasse and moved into the closed ghetto in the suburb of Kamionka. The last entry in Rutka's diary is April 24. More than two years later, after the war ended, Stanislawa returned to Rutka's apartment and found it empty, dilapidated and plundered. The diary, which comprised 60 handwritten pages, was in the assigned hiding place underneath the staircase. It had survived almost in its entirety, except for a few pages—perhaps Rutka herself had torn them out. A few fragments had been erased or possibly damaged by moisture. In addition, a few detached pages were inserted at the end of the notebook. Their contents do not belong to the timeframe of the events Rutka describes in the beginning of 1943 and are not part of the diary as such.

Rutka's Notebook The journal was hidden beneath the stairs of the Laskier apartment in Bedzin and survived the end of the war intact, with some damage from moisture.

Sapinska took the diary and kept it. She read it from time to time and remembered Rutka. When she turned 80, she told her family about the diary, and her nephew became convinced that the diary was of historical value and should be given to the Bedzin municipal museum. The diary, kept in a simple notebook, was handed over to Adam Szydlowski, a chronicler of Jewish life in Bedzin. He started to investigate Rutka's life and to look for survivors of the family. Eventually, Adam contacted me through Bedzin native Lior and through Rutka's cousin Dalia Hampel, whose mother was the sister of Rutka's mother Dvorah (Hampel) Laskier.

During my journey in Rutka's footsteps I met, among others, Linka Gold, Rutka's good friend who today lives in London. She told me about their lives before the war and in the ghetto, and how they both managed to escape from the Aug. 12, 1942, *Aktion* in Bedzin, the mass gathering in which Jews were sorted out by German authorities and assigned destinies of life, labor or extermination. [Rutka writes about this event in the diary.] Linka showed me her school "autograph book," in which there was a note handwritten by Rutka.

In May 2006, I visited Bedzin together with my husband. We followed Rutka's and the Laskier family's footsteps in the streets of Bedzin, guided by Adam Szydlowski, and we visited the homes in which the family had lived before the war and in the ghetto. I shuffled up the staircase of the house in which the diary was hidden, and I sat on the bench in the yard where Stanislawa and Rutka used to meet and talk. I imagined how the wide world of the adolescent, curious, beautiful and talented Rutka closed in on her until the bitter end.

On May 3, 2006, the Polish edition of the diary was launched with a distinguished ceremony in Bedzin's municipal theater, in the presence of the Israeli ambassador and the mayor. In the audience were girls and boys of Rutka's age at the time of her death. I was the guest of honor. Many Internet sites in Poland now tell Rutka's story, and youngsters write poems about her. The Poles have nicknamed Rutka "the Polish Anne Frank"; the city of Bedzin boasts a memorial to her life; and when I imagine the murder pit of my family, of my sister, I feel the pain I took upon myself in fulfilling her desire that her story be told, a burden I carry with honor and love. ❖

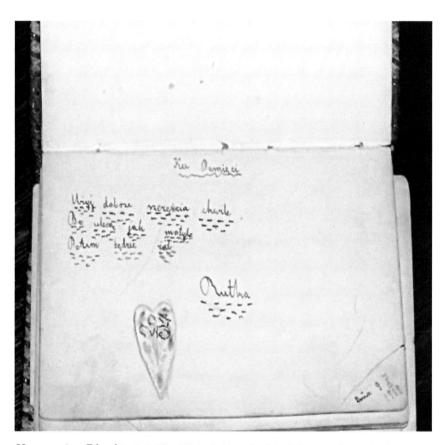

Message to a Friend Rutka's friend Linka Gold survived the Holocaust. Among her keepsakes from the harrowing years of World War II is her autograph book, a page of which was inscribed by Rutka. Linka translated her words as reading: "Enjoy life now, because it flies away very quickly."

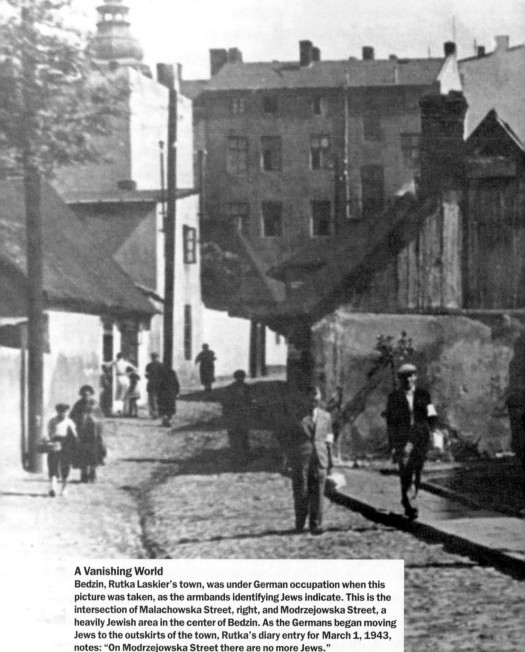

Rutka's Notebook
January-April 1943 • Bedzin, Poland

A Vanishing World
Bedzin, Rutka Laskier's town, was under German occupation when this picture was taken, as the armbands identifying Jews indicate. This is the intersection of Malachowska Street, right, and Modrzejowska Street, a heavily Jewish area in the center of Bedzin. As the Germans began moving Jews to the outskirts of the town, Rutka's diary entry for March 1, 1943, notes: "On Modrzejowska Street there are no more Jews."

January 19, 1943

I cannot grasp that it is already 1943, four years since this hell began. The days pass by quickly; each day looks just like the previous one. Every day it's the same frozen and oppressive boredom. There is great excitement in town. A lot of people are about to leave for "the land of our forefathers," to Palestine. Among these happy people are Syma, Bomek and Ran. I don't know how to explain the feeling that overcame me when I learned about it. It must have been mixed feelings of joy and jealousy. We too live in the hope of getting papers. I think that if this happens, I will be extremely sad to leave Bedzin. As if I am unconsciously curious to know what will happen here ...

I am now reading a wonderful book called *Julian, the Apostate*, and *The Grave of the Unknown Soldier* by Strug. This book reflects my thoughts. I want to completely immerse myself in books, in good, philosophical books. One of the books that really got on my nerves was *The Golem* by Gustav Meyerink. It was a story about the visions of Golem, a man who had lost his mind. I don't really know whether I believe in ghosts or not. In moments of great anxiety, faith in things that are beyond this world is my rock I can lean on. I like to think about matters concerning the afterlife and other mysterious thoughts.

The Laskier Family, 1939
Rutka's family posed for a picture—perhaps taken by her mother Dvorah, who is not shown—in the spring or summer of the year the war broke out. Yaacov Laskier, Rutka's father, is at rear; his mother Golda, who lived with the family, is at left. In 1939, Rutka was 10 years old; she is holding her brother Henius, then 2. Only Yaacov survived the war.

Deliverance Denied

Rutka's joy for her relatives' escape was premature. Her aunt and uncle, Syma and Bomek, and their son Ran, did not succeed in leaving Bedzin, and they later perished, victims of the Holocaust.

Rutka's Library

The authors Rutka was reading in 1943 were popular favorites in Europe in the first decades of the 20th century. Andrzej Strug was the pen name of Tadeusz Galecki (1871-1937), a Polish political theorist, writer and activist. The Grave of the Unknown Soldier *was published in 1922. Julian, the Apostate (1894), was written by Dmitri Sergeyevich Merezhkovsky (1865-1941), the Russian symbolist who opposed Bolshevism and became a follower of Adolf Hitler in later life. The tales of Austrian writer Gustav Meyerink (or Meyrink, 1868-1932) are often imbued with fantasy and horror. His popular 1915 novel* The Golem *is based on a Jewish legend of a manlike creature animated from clay, much like Dr. Frankenstein's Monster. The tale was first told about the Maharal of Prague, Rabbi Judah Loew, in the 16th century.*

January 25, 1943

Nothing. As usual. Every day is the same, except that Mom gets more upset and screams at me because of Henius. This little mischief-maker is very sweet and at the same time very obnoxious. You cannot speak in front of him about anything because he tells everything to the old folks. I have nothing to read. With Mulek everything is OK, I am very pleased about that. Yesterday I went to visit Lolek.

Evening. Micka came to me. We went out and had a drink. I like her, almost love her. The matter with Mulek has gotten complicated again. He thinks that he is being spied upon. Tomorrow I will have a word with him about it. I almost forgot: today I saw Lusia, alive. She's so indifferent. Tomorrow I will also have to settle things with Janek. I'll tell him that if he wants to be my friend, he has to be on time, or else *adios!* Obviously, not in these words exactly. I couldn't care less about him. But I'm curious to see the look on his face. I'm going to sleep.

Morning, January 26, 1943

Micka came again with loads of news. Somebody told her I had cut my hair in order to please Janek, that I had put on silk stockings for Janek, and so on. That's a total lie. As if I even

Henius Laskier
Above, Rutka's younger brother in a 1939 portrait; his full name was Henius-Joachim. He was sent to Auschwitz with Rutka and their mother in August 1943, where he was murdered.

Growing Up in Wartime

In this entry we begin to meet Rutka's circle of adolescent friends, including girlfriends Micka and Lusia and male friends Lolek and Janek. The names are common; historians in Bedzin and at Yad Vashem in Israel have not yet identified these individuals by their family names or in determining their fate. Like most of the Jews in Bedzin, they very likely perished in the Holocaust. It appears that Rutka may have heard a rumor that Lusia had already been sent to a concentration camp but was mistaken.

Notes on the Text

Most of Rutka Laskier's entries do not contain paragraphs; the editors have inserted paragraphs in many entries and have converted the date headers of the individual entries to U.S. usage, but have made minimal changes to the text. The few illegible words are indicated by brackets and an ellipsis mark: [...].

cared about him. If I meet Tusia on the street, I'll ask her who allowed her to spread such gossip, and remind her about a certain little incident that occurred on the night between January 2 and 3. I want to shut her up with these meetings; I wonder how it will turn out. I'm going to the photographer today. I'll have my picture taken for 5 marks, on the account [of future payment].

January 27, 1943

Today I'm in a strange mood. As if I am seized by joy, I am flooded with some kind of happiness I can't explain. As if I was soaked with all the happiness, all the immeasurable distances, and most importantly, I am not homesick. On other days, I am completely absorbed with a longing for something beautiful, wonderful and distant. I feel I would have been relieved if I had had the opportunity to stay in a beautiful place, staring at a wonderful landscape. When I'm standing by the riverside and looking at a gushing waterfall, I feel something inside of me being lifted and taken far away …

I already had my photo taken. I wonder if it looks good. Although usually I don't look pretty in photographs, in reality I am very beautiful. I'll give you a detailed description of my body. Well, I'm tall, thin, with pretty nice legs, very

Poland, 1943

Riga · LATVIA

· Copenhagen · *Baltic Sea* · LITHUANIA

DENMARK

Vilnius ·

· Danzig · East Prussia

· Minsk · WHITE RUSSIA

POLAND 2008 BORDER

POLAND 1939 BORDER

Treblinka ☠

· Berlin

☠ Chelmno · Warsaw · Soblbor ☠ · NAZI/SOVIET DEMARCATION LINE SEPT. 1939

GERMANY

Majdanek ☠

Bedzin ● · Belzec ☠ · UKRAINE

· Prague · ☠ · Krakow
Auschwitz

Protectorate of Bohemia and Moravia

SLOVAK REPUBLIC

· Vienna · Bratislava · HUNGARY · ROMANIA

·Budapest · ——— 75 miles

ITALY
YUGOSLAVIA

■ Germany   □ Other Axis powers
■ Annexed by Germany   □ Other occupied areas
□ General Government   ■ Neutral
☠ Major German death camps in Poland

Poland Under German Occupation

Adolf Hitler's Germany invaded western Poland on Sept. 1, 1939, touching off World War II. As the *blitzkrieg* rolled through Poland, Bedzin was occupied by German troops on Sept. 5, 1939. On September 17, under the terms of the secret August, 1939, agreement between Germany and the U.S.S.R., the Soviets invaded eastern Poland. The country was essentially partitioned for two years, but after Germany invaded the Soviet Union in June, 1941, all of Poland returned to German control. Rutka Laskier's town, Bedzin, and its immediate region were annexed into the Reich and named East Upper Silesia, while occupied northern and eastern Poland, including Warsaw and Krakow, was referred to as the General Government.

MAP BY JOE LERTOLA, TIME

13

thin at the waist, I've got elongated hands but ugly, or more accurately, uncared-for fingernails. I have big black eyes, thick brown eyebrows and long eyelashes, even very long. Black hair, trimmed short and combed back, small but pug nose, nicely outlined lips, snow-white teeth—and there's my portrait.

I would like to pour out on paper all the turmoil I am feeling inside, but I'm absolutely incapable. And now I'll describe my spiritual side as well. They say I'm smart, educated—that could be, although I never studied, that is I didn't do my utmost. I have my nuttiness. Sometimes I am so depressed, that when I open my mouth it's only in order to sting someone. I love stinging people very much but I do it moderately, because as they say, physical bruises close up, but emotional wounds keep on bleeding.

Other days, like today for instance, I am bursting with joy and could laugh all day long. Besides, I'm probably eccentric because I like telling people in the face exactly what I think about them, something not recommended to do in public. I also sometimes like to dress in a crazy manner; for instance, I once went outside in pants. Basically, I couldn't care less. I am who I am and nothing could possibly change that. See you later, my diary.

"And There's My Portrait"
In this undated photograph of Rutka and her mother Dvorah, the young girl—dark-eyed, intense of expression and already a bit gangly—gives promise of meeting her description of herself as an adolescent in her notebook entry at left.

This photograph was attached to the Page of Testimony *(see p. 65)* filed by Yaacov Laskier with Yad Vashem in Israel in 1955.

January 28, 1943

I am stupid, terribly stupid. Yesterday evening, when Nina and I walked by the old Market Square, I met Micka. She was walking with Rozka and Minda. I said "Micka," and although she clearly heard me, she didn't respond and kept on walking. I cannot forgive myself for calling her. Now, between her and me, it's over—*finito*. Besides, I prefer Nina; she's easier to confide in. She came over this evening. We went out. After 7 o'clock I went with her out to buy yeast opposite Lolek's house. She went to buy yeast and I waited by the gate. Jumek and Matek passed by. They saw me and stopped. They asked me whether I was waiting for Janek. Fools, they could've really thought so, but "fortunately" Nina came back.

Tomorrow I plan on going to Lolek to borrow books. At least like that it doesn't look like I'm going to Tusia's apartment. I couldn't care less about anybody, except for Mietek, Nina and maybe Janek, but since Tuesday he hasn't shown up: that's strange. Actually, I'm pretty pleased about that because this way I'm relieved from the discussions, or more accurately questions, asked by the maid. People have such old-fashioned ideas on friendship between adolescent boys and girls. They are incapable of grasping the new world. By tomorrow, I still need to think about going there: should I wait by the factory or go to the apartment? I'll probably meet

Rutka and Danusia, 1932
Yaacov Laskier was a well-to-do banker; his family enjoyed skiing vacations in the winter, hiking in the mountains in the spring and visits to seaside resorts in the summer. Above, Rutka and her friend Danusia, who is mentioned in the notebook, enjoy an outing in 1932. Rutka, then age 3, is in the pilot's seat. Both girls perished in the Holocaust.

the whole gang there. I couldn't care less about them; all that matters to me is getting the books. I'll go with Nina after seven o'clock.

All right, enough with the writing for now. I notice that I feel very reassured, as if I confessed to someone. I wonder if Jewish women are allowed to confess to a Christian priest. Whom can I ask about it?

January 29, 1943

Janek didn't come …

January 30, 1943

Today a hundred demons are running wild inside of me. I met Micka and we talked about our lives in the future. In the morning I made an appointment with Janek and Micka to meet at 4:30 p.m. I returned home from Mietek before 4 o'clock, and I was told Janek had already been here and left. He will probably not come again. Micka didn't come either. How can you not go crazy? Now everything is messed up. I just don't know what's going on with me. Micka may arrive any moment and Dad is at home; everything has gotten very complicated. Sometimes all the "disasters" happen at once.

What shall I do now? How will I get in touch with them

Bedzin Teens, 1941
A group of Jewish students at the Furstenburg School in Bedzin enjoy a graduation outing in 1941. Rutka Laskier also attended the school until the Germans closed all the Jewish schools in Bedzin, and she may well have known some of these students, who were a few years older. Genia Prawer, in the front row at left, survived the Holocaust after a harrowing series of escapes from German authorities. Heniek Lewin, whose face is largely obscured in the middle of the center row, may be the "Heniek" Rutka refers to in her diary.

again? With Micka and Janek. Wow, I'm so furious. Especially at Janek. Instead of 4:30 p.m. he comes at 3:30 p.m.; he didn't come for such a long time because he was ashamed. His boots were taken away, therefore he goes with [...]

Janek has just arrived at this moment and has left immediately, promising to return soon. Right now, in the morning, I'm in a sweet mood [...]

I'd very much like to

31.1. 43 nothing

1.2 nothing

2.2 nothing

3.2 nothing

4.2 nothing

February 5, 1943

The rope around us is getting tighter and tighter. Next month there should already be a ghetto, a real one, surrounded by walls. In the summer it will be unbearable.

A Street in the Ghetto, 1942
Most of Bedzin's Jews lived in the center of town, above, which grew increasingly crowded as the German occupation continued and Jews from other areas of Poland were relocated in the city. By early 1943, German authorities began moving Jews to the outskirts of Bedzin, creating a new, more closely supervised ghetto in the rundown district of Kamionka, as Rutka notes.

"Nothing" Doing

> *On five consecutive days near the beginning of February, Rutka wrote only the date and "nothing." She generally spelled out the name of the month but did not do so in these cases, suggesting that she may have written the numeric dates on February 5, keeping track of the days.*

To sit in a gray locked cage, without being able to see fields and flowers. Last year I used to go to the fields; I always had many flowers, and it reminded me that one day it would be possible to go to Malachowska Street without taking the risk of being deported. Being able to go to the cinema in the evening. I'm already so "flooded" with the atrocities of the war that even the worst reports have no effect on me. I simply can't believe that one day I'll be able to leave the house without the yellow star. Or even that this war will end one day … If this happens, I will probably lose my mind from joy.

But now I need to think about the near future, which is the ghetto. Then it will be impossible to see anyone, neither Micka, who lives in Kamionka C, nor Janek, who lives in D, and not Nica, who lives in D. And then what will happen?

Oh, good Lord. Well, Rutka, you've probably gone completely crazy. You are calling upon God as if He exists. The little faith I used to have has been completely shattered. If God existed, He would have certainly not permitted that human beings be thrown alive into furnaces, and the heads of little toddlers be smashed with butts of guns or be shoved into sacks and gassed to death … It sounds like a fairy tale. Those who haven't seen this would never believe it. But it's not a legend; it's the truth. Or the time when they beat an old man until he became unconscious, because he didn't

From Auschwitz to Bedzin

In the first years of the occupation of Poland, the Germans deported some Jews out of the town of Auschwitz (Oscwiecim in Polish) and settled them in Bedzin, as shown above. After Birkenau, the extermination camp at Auschwitz, became fully operational in 1943, the journey was reversed, and thousands of Jews from Bedzin were sent there to be murdered.

Malachowska Street

This was a main street in Bedzin that the Germans forbade the Jews to use; it was later used as part of the deportation route for the town's Jews.

Kamionka Ghetto

Early in the occupation of Bedzin, the Germans maintained the large Jewish neighborhood in the city's center as an "open" ghetto; there were no walls sealing off the Jewish quarter, and traffic moved freely between the ghetto and the rest of the city. But in 1943 the Germans established a new ghetto in the shabby Kamionka district on the outskirts of town. This was a "closed" ghetto, with guards restricting ingress and egress. As Rutka anticipated, the Laskiers were moved from the open ghetto to Kamionka late in April 1943, when her entries in the notebook cease. At left, Rutka was apparently concerned that the heightened restrictions on travel would sever her connection with her friends, some of whom were already living in alphabetized quadrants in Kamionka.

23

cross the street properly. This is already absurd; it's nothing, as long as there won't be Auschwitz ... and a green card ... The end ... When will it come? ...

February 6, 1943

Something has broken in me. When I pass by a German, everything shrinks in me. I don't know whether it is out of fear or hatred. I would like to torture them, their women and children, who set their doggies on us, to beat and strangle them vigorously, more and more. When will this day arrive which Nica talked about ... that's one matter.

And now another matter. I think my womanhood has awoken in me. That means, yesterday when I was taking a bath and the water stroked my body, I longed for someone's hands to stroke me ... I didn't know what it was, I have never had such sensations until now ...

I met Micka today. I don't know with what these "dubious" lovers attract her, to the point that she refuses to get into a quarrel with them. They are so dazzled by her and think that every boy should be in love with her. Of course, I ascribe this to Janek, but Janek finds her disgusting (I don't know why). I think Janek likes me very much. But it doesn't matter to me, either way.

Today, I recalled in detail the day of August 12, 1942, the

The Children of Auschwitz

The Polish children above were numbered and photographed after arriving at Auschwitz in 1942. By 1943 most of the Jewish children who arrived at the camp were immediately sent to the gas chambers in the Birkenau sector of the camp; this is believed to have been Rutka Laskier's fate. It is significant that early in 1943 Rutka and her circle of friends suspected that Jews were being slaughtered on a mass scale at the Auschwitz-Birkenau camp, suggesting that such information was sometimes shared among Poland's Jews.

Green Card

This entry is confusing; generally, Jews who received green cards were recognized as possessing "special abilities" and were thus not condemned to the death camps. Recipients of such cards were often scientists or armaments experts. Rutka may simply have confused the meaning of the term; she clearly believes a green card amounts to a death sentence.

Hakoah. I'll try to describe that day so that in a few years, of course if I'm not deported, I'll be able to remember it. We got up at four o'clock in the morning. We had a great breakfast (considering it was wartime): eggs, salad, real butter, coffee with milk. When we were completely ready, it was already half past five, and then we left. There were thousands of people on the road. Every once in a while we had to stop, in order to let the crowd in front of us proceed.

At half past six, we were in place. We managed to get quite good seats on a bench. We were in a pretty good mood until nine o'clock. Then I looked beyond the fence and I saw soldiers with machine guns aimed at the square in case someone tried to escape (how could you possibly escape from here?). People fainted, children cried. In short— Judgment Day.

People were thirsty, and there was not a single drop of water around. It was terribly hot. Then, all of a sudden, it started pouring. The rain didn't stop. At three o'clock Kuczynsky arrived and the selection started. "1" meant returning home, "1a" meant going to labor, which was even worse than deportation, "2" meant going for further inspection, and "3" meant deportation, in other words, death.

Then I saw what disaster meant. We reported for selection at four o'clock [p.m.]. Mom, Dad and my little brother were sent to group 1, and I was sent to 1a. I walked as if I were

Moving Day
Early in 1943 the Germans began moving Jews from the open ghetto in Bedzin, above, to the closed ghetto in Kamionka, on the southeast side of town, where quarters were so tight that household possessions were often left behind. Only months later, in August 1943, almost all the residents of the Kamionka ghetto were sent to Auschwitz to be executed.

The *Aktion* at Hakoah

The sport field of the Hakoah soccer team in Bedzin's neighboring town of Sosnowiec was the location of the German Aktion, or sorting out, of the city's Jews. In this grisly procedure, Jews were divided into distinct groups, a process that amounted to being handed a sentence of life or death.

Kuczynsky

SS-Obersturmführer Friedrich Kucznysky (1914–1948) was the local German overseer of the Jewish Order Service, the Jews enlisted to police the ghettos. He was employed by the Schmelt organization, the corporation established by Hitler's deputy Heinrich Himmler that was responsible for the "employment of foreigners"—Jews performing slave labor—in East Upper Silesia. Kuczynsky was brought before a Polish court in 1948, charged with committing crimes against the Jews. He was convicted and sentenced to death.

stunned. Salek Goldzweig, Linka Gold, Niania Potocka already sat there. The weirdest thing was that we didn't cry at all, AT ALL. We didn't shed a single tear. Later on, I saw many more disasters. I can't put it in words. Little children were lying on the wet grass, the storm raging above our heads. The policemen beat them ferociously and also shot them.

I sat there until one o'clock at night. Then I ran away. My heart pounded. I jumped out of a window from the first floor of a small building, and nothing happened to me. Only my lips were bitten so bad that they bled. I was completely torn apart. When I was already on the street, I ran into someone "in uniform," and I felt that I couldn't take it anymore. My head was spinning. I was pretty sure he was going to beat me ... but apparently he was drunk and didn't see the "yellow star," and he let me go.

Around me it was dark like in a closed cabin. From time to time flashes of lightning lightened the sky ... and it thundered. The journey that normally takes me half an hour I did in ten minutes. Everybody was at home except Grandma, whom Dad released and brought home the next day. That was everything.

Oh, I forgot the most important thing. I saw how a soldier tore a baby, who was only a few months old, out of its mother's hands and bashed his head against an electric

The Yellow Star
Across Nazi-controlled Europe, including the Third Reich and its Axis allies, Jews were forced to wear identifying marks, usually yellow stars, often worn on armbands. It wasn't a new idea: Muslim and Christian rulers had intermittently forced Jews to wear distinguishing articles of clothing, usually belts and hats, since at least the 9th century. For the Nazis, making the Jews identifiable by such symbols, which became mandatory in Poland soon after the Nazi occupation, was a further step toward distinguishing them as outcasts. Later Jews were herded into isolated districts and ultimately to extermination, the "Final Solution."

Salek and Linka
Salek Goldzweig, Rutka's friend, shared her fate: she was murdered in Auschwitz in 1943. Paulinka (Linka) Gold, Rutka's school friend, survived the Holocaust and eventually settled in London. Rutka's inscription in her school autograph book is shown on p. 5.

pylon. The baby's brain splashed on the wood. The mother went crazy.

I am writing this as if nothing has happened. As if I were in an army experienced in cruelty. But I'm young, I'm 14, and I haven't seen much in my life, and I'm already so indifferent. Now I am terrified when I see "uniforms." I'm turning into an animal waiting to die. One can lose one's mind thinking about this.

Now to everyday matters: Janek came by this afternoon. We had to sit in the kitchen. I got on his nerves and I told him that I had given away all my photographs. He got very upset. We were joking around; we spoke about "Nica and the gang." While we were talking he suddenly blurted out he'd like it very much if he could kiss me. I said "maybe" and continued the conversation. He was a bit confused; he thought I was Tusia or Hala Zelinger. I would have allowed [myself] to be kissed only by the person I loved, and I feel indifferent towards him.

Then Dad sent me to deal with something. I had to leave. Janek accompanied me. While going downstairs I asked him, is kissing such a pleasant thing? And then I told him that I had already kissed before, what a taste it has (that's completely true). He burst out laughing. (He has a nice laugh, I must admit.) He said he was curious too. Maybe, but I won't let him kiss me. I'm afraid it would destroy

"I'm Terrified when I See 'Uniforms' "

Rutka's fear of uniforms was justified. At the same time she was writing her diary, Jews in the Warsaw Ghetto were rising up against their German jailers. In a bloody, courageous stand against enormous odds, the vastly outnumbered fighters of the Warsaw Ghetto managed to stand off the German troops for weeks. The rebellion ended in May, 1943, with the eradication of the vast majority of Jews in the ghetto. Above, mothers and children are arrested, in a photograph included in German commander Jürgen Stroop's report on the revolt to Adolf Hitler.

something beautiful, pure … I'm also afraid that I'll be very disappointed.

February 15, 1943, Monday

I haven't written in a while. And there was nothing to write about. Maybe just the fact that the Germans have retreated from the Eastern front, which may signal the nearing of the end of the war. I'm only afraid that we, the Jews, will be finished before. They retreated from Krasnodar, Stalingrad, Novorossiysk and now they are retreating from Kharkov.

But how shrewd am I, I have written already so much about the war and nothing about myself. Janek hasn't been seen since Wednesday. I must admit that I miss him, I mean, not him but his forehead. He has a wonderful white forehead. If he doesn't come today either, then I will wait for him in front of "Wariat."

I would like to know what's with Nica. Jumek gave Mietek a photograph of Tusia. I'm curious if Jumek is still in love with Tusia. Actually, he's a good guy. I like him, but not in the same way I like Mietek. With Mulek you can talk and forget about the sex difference, and I like that very much. When you talk to Janek, he is always very polite, reserved, just waiting for the moment he can help me with some-

At Last, Hitler's War Machine Retreats

As Rutka notes in her February 15 entry, the great turning point in World War II on Europe's Eastern front was the Russians' successful defense of besieged Stalingrad in February 1943. At its conclusion, 91,000 German troops were captured and Hitler's armies began a long, slow withdrawal toward Germany. Above, German troops are marched to prison camps; only 5,000 of those taken captive are believed to have survived and returned to their homeland.

"Wariat"

> *The word means "crazy" or "insane" in Polish. It is probably a nickname for a place visited by Rutka and her circle, but its meaning is unknown.*

thing and in that way, show me his superiority. Oh, him and his superiority! I can't stand it, that's why I liked Lolek. Actually, I still like him, but I haven't seen him in a while.

I plan to go to Lolek in order to get the book "P.P." I heard it's great. It would be a great opportunity also to talk with Tuska about Rozka. I hate those two; I hate Rozka even more than Tuska. I had an argument with Tuska but it was for her own good. I saw how jealous she was (though at that time I didn't understand that). She was afraid to leave me alone in the room with Janek. I made a scene and we fell out. She was basically very pleased with it. And one more thing: I have decided to let Janek kiss me. Eventually, someone will kiss me for the first time, so let it be Janek. I do like him.

February 17, 1943

Finally, I got in touch with Nica. We're meeting today at 5:15 p.m. at Jumek's. I'm happy because not only will it "take place," but also because I'll see Janek. It's interesting that the less I see him the more I like him. I wonder what we'll be reading about with Nica. I wanted to visit Jumek but on my way back from the community [house], I met him. And another thing: maybe I'll have the opportunity to see and meet Heini Wajnsztok, whom I have heard a lot about, in connection with Malgorzata and Tusia. I wonder if

Notebook Page
This is Rutka's diary entry for January 27, 1943. In the majority of her entries she does not divide her text into paragraphs.

❖

"Rozka"

    This is most likely Rozka Rechnic; see the note on p. 41.

"P.P." and the Community House

    The title of the book Rutka refers to as "P.P." is not known. At this point in the German occupation, the Jewish schools in Bedzin had been shut down, and Jewish youngsters would often get together in groups of three to four and lstudy in hiding. It is possible that Rutka is writing here about such a meeting.

he's as handsome as everybody says. I also have to go to Lolek's in order to get books; I can't delay it. Lately I am very absent-minded.

February 20, 1943

I have a feeling that I'm writing for the last time. There is an Aktion in town. I'm not allowed to go out and I'm going crazy, imprisoned in my own house. I wanted to go to Jumek and warn him about the Aktion. Hopefully, he wasn't caught.

For a few days, something's in the air. Yesterday there was an "Ausrottungskommission" in Chrzanow. It's expected also to happen here. The town is breathlessly waiting in anticipation, and this anticipation is the worst of all. I wish it would end already! This is torment; this is hell. I try to escape from these thoughts, of the next day, but they keep haunting me like nagging flies. If only I could say, it's over, you die only once ... But I can't, because despite all these atrocities I want to live, and wait for the following day. That means, waiting for Auschwitz or labor camp.

I must not think about this so now I'll start writing about private matters. I was hopelessly foolish about Janek. Now my eyes have been opened. I wised up. Just like that, without speaking or even seeing him. He's a disgusting type of

Arrival of Deported Jews in Bedzin
Above, Jews from Auschwitz (Oswiecim) arrive in Bedzin; the number of Jews swelled in the city as refugees from other areas of Poland joined these local deportees in settling here.

"Ausrottungskommission"

There was, in fact, no "Ausrottungskommission" (extermination commission). In general, deportation operations from a locality were often organized with assistance from German authorities from outside that town. Local SS, police commanders and German civilian authorities would meet with the commanders of the incoming deportation unit(s) a day or two before a planned deportation from a town or city, in order to prepare the operation. It is possible that in some places, Jews began to take notice of the arrival of SS people from outside and their conferring with local German officials, which was followed by a deportation Aktion. Jews might have called this arrival of outsiders and the German meeting an "Ausrottungskommission." Such a preparatory meeting took place in Chrzanow on February 18, 1943, and Rutka's reference to this two days later reflects the fact that information and rumors traveled quickly from town to town.

Chrzanow

The seat of a county southeast of Bedzin.

YAD VASHEM

guy, one of those who kill in white gloves. And he's not smart either. The only thing that matters to him is that his pants are ironed, how many cakes he ate at Frontag's coffee house, and the nice legs of the girls. He's very hypocritical. Anyways, he's definitely not a Communist, and I don't understand why Lolek pulled him into this. He can only do harm. A despicable person.

Jumek is another story. He's got common sense, and a highly intelligent and practical nature. He's very devoted to Nica and company. Without elaborating, I like him very much. We planned that we would go to Tusia and tell her everything, and with that we'll shut her big mouth. She knows too much and chatters too much. Maybe I'll also go to Jumek, I'd like to very much. Rutka, why are you putting it into your head that you hate him?

February 24, 1943

There is a temporary remission of tension in town. Who knows what will happen? There is talk of general departure to labor, "Arbeitsamt." For men and women aged between 16–50. Once again they hunt Communists. I don't know when I'll meet Nica.

Oh yes ... On Saturday afternoon Micka came over. We went out. We met with Jumek and Mietek. Had a stroll with

"Arbeitsamt"

The term means "labor bureau"; here it refers to the Judenrat, the group that allocated Jews for work duty at the demand of the Germans. The gates of Auschwitz, which was used primarily as a labor camp, read *ARBEIT MACHT FREI:* "Work will make you free." But by 1943 another part of the complex, Birkenau, had become an extermination center, where Jews were gassed, then burned in crematoria, above. This was Rutka's fate.

"... why Lolek pulled him into this ..."

> Rutka's meaning is not clear. She may have been writing about the secret Jewish studying groups or about the underground activities of the Gordonia youth movement, of which she was a member. Perhaps Rutka had ties with the underground. Stanislawa Sapinska, the keeper of the notebook, suspected she did.

them and then we went to Mietek's. On the way we met Janek in his brown suit. He came up to me and asked me where I was going. I told him that we were taking a walk. He asked if the rest of the gang was going as well. I nodded … He was very perplexed. Finally he decided to join us. Then he talked with Jumek. They stayed behind. Then I turned back and asked: "Are you coming, Jumek?"

Janek blushed. He asked with a forced smile: "So I don't mean anything to you anymore?" He shook my hand, only mine, and said good-bye. God, he's so disgusting! Then I met Salek Saper. A nice guy.

Things with Mom are getting more and more complicated. Yesterday she saw me with Jumek, Mietek and Micka. Mom tried to get a confession out of me. She doesn't understand that it's difficult for me to open my heart to an adult. Maybe I could confide in Micka, but not everything. Lately, I love my parents even more. But sometimes they are so mean to me, it hurts me so much, and then I become hurtful and bad. Tusia and her grandpa were here earlier, and asked where Gichu lives. They probably went to Erich. While her grandpa was talking with Mom, I asked her what has she said to Rozka Rechnic. She said I abandoned her and speak only to Lolek. That's not nice of her, because she knows I can't apologize, because if I did, I'd have to tell Nica. I just wanted to tell her that, when Mom walked in. Tusia said

Rozka Rechnic

The reference is not clear. Rutka appears to be writing about a different person than the Rozka (Ickowitz) Rechnic, wife of Leon Rechnic, who survived the Holocaust, immigrated to the U.S. in 1946 and told her story in the book Try to Survive: And Tell the World *(Real Press, 2002) before her death in 2006.*

Rutka's Parents

Like adolescents in every era, Rutka clashed with her parents. At left are Dvorah and Yaacov Laskier early in their marriage. Below, the two enjoy a ski holiday in Zakopane, the mountain resort city in southern Poland, in 1930.

good-bye and left. She thought that I wanted to reconcile with her. What a fool! Although I know I can't stand Janek, I still like to hear what they say about him ... Today I'll probably meet with Jumek and Micka. I wonder if he was at Micka's.

March 1, 1943

Once again I took a long break from writing, during which we managed to reduce our apartment to one room. It's very crowded. Nobody knows where to find things. Yesterday I met Jumek. I told him to come. So he came today. We talked. Micka was there too. Then we went downstairs and met Janek, Lolek, Numek and Tadek. Janek came up to me and told me that he hasn't seen me for a while. Then he added that he'll come to visit me. He tried to speak at ease but he couldn't. Tomorrow evening I'll meet Jumek.

It's so boring at home: boring and there's nowhere to go to. On Modrzejowska Street there are no more Jews. Today we reported to the commission. I'll work at the Sammlung-werkstätte des Sonderbeauftragten. That is the safest factory. I plan to invite Jumek, Janek and Micka on Saturday. We'll sit in the small room. Enough writing for today.

And another thing, I saw Heini Wajnsztok. I already imagined he would look like Apollo, and he's just a pale

9

Alfred Rossner

Lohnstepperei

Bendzin O/S.

Fernsprecher Nr. 71578.

Bank für Stadt u. Land} Konto
Kreissparkasse, Bendzin} Nr. 364

Bendzin, den 1. März 1941
Fabrikstr. 37.

Betrifft.

B e s c h e i n i g u n g.

Die bei Herrn/Frau......Prawer Liba, Hinter dem Wall 2
stehende Maschine.Nähmaschine......Marke.Veritas.......Nr. 2295629
ist für meinem Betrieb reserviert.

i.A.

Alfred Rossner Certificate

The document above is a certificate issued by Alfred Rossner, the industrialist in whose "shop" Rutka was sent to work, stating that a sewing machine located in the apartment of Luba Prawer in Bedzin had been reserved for use by the Rossner workshops. Luba Prawer was the mother of Genia Prawer, whose picture can be seen on p. 19.

❖

"Sammlungwerkstätte des Sonderbeauftragten"

The term means "Workshop Gathered by the Special Commissioners." Rutka is probably referring to Alfred Rossner's uniform-seaming factory. Rossner's "shops" were considered the safest factories in which to work, as Rutka notes; the German industrialist, like the better-known Oskar Schindler, was sympathetic to his Jewish employees and worked to shield them from deportation and the death camps.

guy with a barber's face, and with nicely combed hair.

March 7, 1943

I don't understand why I can't pour out my heart even on paper. It's very difficult to self-analyze. I'm persuading myself that I'm not in love with Janek, but in the meantime I miss him, and sometimes I suffer because I don't see him and hear his voice. Sometimes I regret I was so cold towards him. I laughed at him until he bit his lips and bled...

> And what was yesterday is gone,
> what was yesterday
> I remained alone in the evening in the fields
> My troubles suddenly disappeared.
> When was it? Yesterday?
> His lips kissed me,
> kissed me.

Actually I shouldn't feel so hopeless. We didn't even have a fight, but something went wrong that evening when I showed him my photographs with a dedication to Mietek. Then he looked at me with his ugly eyes, stood there for a while and then left. He hasn't been here since. Why? I pretended to be indifferent, but in reality I found it difficult without Janek. Yet, it's not too late. I spoke with Nica and I will see him there.

"I Can't Pour Out My Heart"

Rutka's depression is understandable. Her dreams are often of escape, either into sleep or into visions of pure flight—anywhere to get away from what she describes later in the March 7 entry as "all this grayish rottenness." Above, a ghetto scene on the street where Bedzin's synagogue stood before it was burned down. Bedzin survivor Dasha Rittenberg recalled in 2008: "The Germans took possession of almost everything we owned. The police came into our home and carried away all the furniture. I remember my mother running after them crying, 'What will the children eat on?' "

I wish I could leave all this behind and run away very far from Janek, Jumek, Mietek, my house and all this grayish rottenness. Spread out wings and fly high and far away, hear the wind howling and run wild on my face, feel its breeze. Fly to places where there are no ghettos, "shops," no pretending. And now it's enough, let's go to sleep. There is nothing like sleep, as it says in the poem "The Happy House" [by] [Ch]odasiewicz ...

> Bitter ashes in a sad heart
> Quiet sleep in a dark glass
> Who hasn't drunk from a dark glass
> When bitter ashes are in your heart
> And in the glass lies quiet sleep?

Janek was at my house on February 13, 1943, for the last time. I think I won't ask him to come anymore.

March 8, 1943

What's happening to you, Rutka? You're incapable of controlling yourself. That's not good. I must pull myself together and not wet my pillow with tears. Because of whom or what am I crying? Because of Janek, certainly not. Then because of whom? Probably because of freedom. I am sick and tired of these gray houses, of the steady fear seen on

A Battle with Starvation

As the war dragged on, food and other necessities grew ever more scarce. The woman above appears to be selling food from a tray. According to former Bedzin resident Dasha Rittenberg, "The trouble really started in the winter of 1940. It was a very cold winter, and our food rations were cut …When a piece of bread arrived, my parents would cut it into tiny pieces and always give their children the largest pieces."

"Shops"

> Workshops in which the Jews of the ghetto were forced to toil for low wages. Some, such as Alfred Rossner's workshops in Bedzin, were humane.

"The Happy House"

> It is difficult to decipher the name of the poet. It is very likely the Russian poet Vladislav Chodasiewicz (1886–1939).

47

everybody's faces. This fear clutches on to everyone and doesn't let go. Today, probably Nica, Jumek, Janek will come to me. Damn it, Janek again. I decided not to think about him, but thoughts about him keep coming back. Have I really lost my head because of him? I don't know, is this what they call love?

"Yes, Janek, I fell in love with you, but I made one unforgivable mistake. I fell in love with you while you were gone. I believe you love me too, but you were too proud to come back. I know this from Jumek. When you were at Lolek's, you suddenly got up, put on your coat, and said: 'I'm going to Rutka's.' Then Jumek said: 'Don't go so fast, Rutka said she doesn't enjoy your visits that much.' Apparently you turned pale and were grumpy all evening. Janek, you little fool, you will come back to me. R."

Whoever reads this will take this seriously. I know how to write emotionally.

March 9, 1943

I think I've gone completely crazy. Today when I woke up I realized that not a single drop of fondness for Janek is left in me. I probably persuaded myself like I persuaded myself all the other times when I fell in love, except when I fell in love with Tolek. Tolek already lives in Bedzin; I hope I'll see

A World in Ruins
Occupying Germans organized the Jews of Bedzin into work details; above, laborers are clearing rubble from a collapsed building. At one point, Jewish workers were enlisted in an effort to straighten the path of the river that winds through the town—using picks and shovels.

him this week. My heart is overjoyed; I haven't seen him in a very long time. I miss him very much. Today I was at Hala's; I stayed there until half past 7. Oh, how I wish the war would be over soon. Every day it's the same: I'm sick and tired of it. I'll probably start working next month. I want to learn how to work. To be a Communist and not to work doesn't go together.

Wednesday, March 17, 1943

Nothing special. Within three months we have to move from our house to Kamionka. Actually, that's not the worst. Yesterday I saw Janek on the street. He said hello to me and stopped. I pretended I didn't see him and kept going. I'm so boring. On Sunday I was in Kamionka at Tolek's, but he wasn't at home. It's a pity; I wanted to leave behind Micka, Nina, Hala, etc. Except Tolek. I like him very much. I think he likes me too. I like him, but I'm not losing my mind.

I can't figure it out. To lose one's mind means only physical attraction. That's what happened to Janek. To Janek, Marek, Moniek, etc. That's really silly, I mean, marriage. People are tied up. Everything is full of sex. There is no platonic love or maybe it is covered with friendship. I think that people who really love one another should not get married.

Journey to Kamionka

Jews in the open ghetto in central Bedzin pack up their belongings as they prepare to move to far humbler quarters in the Kamionka district on the outskirts of town. Bedzin survivor Dasha Rittenberg recalls: "Every month, more Jews were pushed into the ghetto and every month the food rations got smaller." Of Kamionka, she says: "This was already a Jewish neighborhood, but it was the poorest Jewish area of Bedzin. A place of terrible, squalid poverty."

March 20, 1943

Today I was assigned to work. On Monday at 6:30 a.m. I already have to be at the factory. Darn, 6:30 is terribly early. If it were at least summer, then it would somehow be possible. I wonder what kind of a job I'll have ...

Tomorrow I'm supposed to meet Tolek. I'm very happy about that. Nowadays we're allowed to walk on [...] and Gzichow. I'm bored. On those two streets hundreds of adolescent girls and boys, and local macho men renowned for their hunting skills, walk around. When I go to Micka I have to go via those two streets. I'm not at all at ease then. These machos undress each girl that passes by with their eyes and measure her from top to bottom. I walk as fast as possible but in spite of that, remarks about my legs and face can't be avoided. Then I don't feel good, a kind of nausea and a sense of brutality. I remember Lolek B. looking at me the same way. It's an extremely unpleasant feeling, like merchandise on the market. I wonder what Tolek looks like. I saw Janek on Thursday when I went to Hala. We walked in the same direction. I couldn't get rid of him. I can't stand him.

April 5, 1943

Well, I've started working. The days go by; every day it's

Men About Town

A group of young men gather outside a house in the Bedzin ghetto; the photo is undated. Their relaxed demeanor suggests that the picture was taken early in the German occupation of Poland; smiles and good cheer grew scarce as the war continued.

Gzichow

A neighborhood in Bedzin notorious as a hotbed of anti-Semitism.

the same, grizzly days. I work from 8 a.m. to 2 p.m. It's tolerable. The work is quite easy, it's working out somehow. I'm extremely tired and I feel like sleeping all the time. Jumek has been deported; Mietek saw him and sent me his regards. I feel very sorry for him. He was a good guy. I don't feel like writing anymore.

April 24

The summer is already here. It's difficult for me to sit still in the "shop." The sun is shining so brightly. Outside the windows apple trees and lilacs are blooming, and you have to sit in this suffocating and stinking room and sew. The hell with it. This week I was in the Srodula ghetto for two days at Suma's. I met a very handsome boy and became reacquainted with my cousin whom I haven't seen in seven years. Those two days went by very fast. I didn't want to return home, but there's no choice. The town is already empty. Almost everyone lives in Kamionka. We will probably move there this week too. Meanwhile I'm very bored. The entire day I'm walking around the room, I have nothing to do.

Inside a "Shop"

This damaged photo shows four Jews working in the office of the Leopold Michatz garment factory in the Bedzin ghetto. From left: Natek Aleksandrowicz, [name missing] Kahane, Hanka Granek and Herko Brukner. Granek survived the Holocaust.

Srodula

A district on the outskirts of nearby Sosnowiec, where a ghetto was established in 1942–43. The Srodula and Kamionka districts eventually merged into a single large ghetto. The "Suma" Rutka refers to has not been identified.

End of Chronology

The April 24 entry is the final dated passage in the notebook. The Laskier family was relocated to the Kamionka ghetto soon after this date. Months later, the Germans liquidated Kamionka and sent its residents to Auschwitz-Birkenau. A fortunate few, like Rutka's father Yaacov, survived.

In the Mountains

At daybreak I got up and ran to the window. A tiny bit of the golden sun was already peeking through the horizon. I dressed up, packed my knapsack, picked up a hiking stick and left. After less than thirty minutes I arrived at the foot of the mountain. I started climbing. From the valley I could hear the murmur of the river mingle with the sound of the church bells. Beyond the branches of the pine trees the mountain peaks appeared.

Along the barely visible path, through the entangled pale bushes and the raspberry bushes and the thorny gooseberry bushes, I climbed higher and higher. I jumped from one stone to another, above trunks of fallen trees; I found my way through the entangled bushes. Before me the peaks of the giant mountains rose. The long weeds wept and covered the slopes. The cowbells sounded like moaning, heard from far away.

More and more often rocks blocked my way, the mass of rocks rose high, piles of rocks, stained here and there with lichens and green-blue moss, and somewhere else, roots of trees were twisted like coiled snakes. The [enveloped] rocks sank under my feet into reddish moss, and when I stepped on them, I gently sank into it. The curled greenery of black-berries and gooseberries stretched out its arms into the

Zakopane Vista
It is impossible to locate the countryside described by Rutka in this undated entry, which may be entirely fanciful and intended as a short story. However, the Laskier family is known to have vacationed in Zakopane, above, in the Polish section of the Carpathian Mountains.

Fragments

> The last two entries in Rutka's notebook are undated fragments written on loose pages and inserted separately into the book. They do not fit into the chronology of the diary.

moss, and above it all, the purple-blue blackberries were sprinkled like dew.

I sat down there. Above me the pine trees were growling and the rustle of the needles merged with the paddling of the stream. The sun flooded the mountain with its golden rays and outlined the green of the grass. In the distance, a thin bluish streak of smoke lit by shepherds could be seen far away ...

August 11, 1942
Winter in the Ghetto

Big flakes of snow are falling and covering the mud on the street with a white layer. Winter. Nevertheless, the usual children's cries of joy announcing the arrival of the winter are not heard on the streets. For most of the ghetto's inhabitants, the winter is a nightmare of terrible poverty and hunger. Everywhere people are standing in line, lines for potatoes, coal, bread. Children dressed in worn-out clothes stretch out their hands to those passing by.

These children are the most predominant symbol of the gray ghetto. The parents have been deported, and the children were left abandoned to their destiny, to go astray in the streets. The people's faces express sadness and worry.

Suddenly there is a scream, a police officer pushed an

Bare Subsistence
A man buys bread from a Bedzin street vendor in the depths of winter. "We were told that we were subhumans, and we were treated as such," recalls Dasha Rittenberg

August 11, 1942

This date was written at the end of this fragment. It could be that Rutka wrote the description of the wedding on that date.

elderly person, he fell and his head hit the road. The white snow soaked up the crimson blood. Over there, a woman is crying, her husband has been imprisoned, who knows if she'll ever see him again …

The church tower's clock indicates it's five o'clock. The "shop" workers pour out onto the streets. Young hungry girls, pale-faced, anemic […]

… The bride broke out in tears all the way to the church. The wedding procession was on its way. On the way they sang and went wild. In the church the priest gave them his blessings and guided them. They proceeded home, where a wonderful banquet awaited them. The sun was already going down when they left the tables. Then the dancing started, followed by the ritual of cutting of the bread. After the headdress ceremony the bride cried bitterly. The headdress ceremony was followed by the traditional dowry ceremony.

Winter Journey
German soldiers march a group of Jews, members of a forced-labor detail, down Modrzejowska Street in Bedzin.

Anemic [...]

> *A few lines of the diary are erased at this point, probably owing to humidity.*
> *The context of the final passage is thus unclear.*

The Three Lives of Yaacov Laskier

By Zahava (Laskier) Scherz

My father Yaacov Laskier, who was born in the year 1900 in Bedzin, Poland, can be said to have experienced three different lives in a single life-span. His first life was rooted deeply in the history of Jews in Poland at the beginning of the 20th century. The Laskier family was among the respected families of Bedzin in the Zaglembie region of Poland. Among the family members were Emanuel Laskier [or Lasker], mathematician and chess champion, and his brother Jonathan, who was married to the poet Else Lasker-Schuler.

My grandfather David Laskier was an affluent Jew who owned a big flour mill and was very religious. He married Golda Zisman, and they had nine children—four girls and five boys, among them my father Yaacov, the fifth child. As was common in those days, my father was sent to Heder, Jewish religious elementary school, when he was 3 years old. However, while he was still young, my father rebelled against traditional religious education and was transferred to the secular high school, some 12 km (7.5 miles) away from his house. He walked this distance daily for four years.

Yaacov, a dedicated violin player, joined the Dror youth movement, which promoted both Zionism and socialism, as a young teen. When he turned 17, during World War I, he ran away to Israel, together with five friends from Bedzin. The "Bedzin Six" made their way from Poland through Odessa to Istanbul, along the way meeting the great Hebrew poet Hayyim Nahman Bialik and the Zionist leader Menahem Ussishkin. They traveled by ship from Turkey to Zionism's Promised Land: Eretz Israel. Then under the control of the Ottoman Empire, this biblical "Land of Israel" became the British Mandate for Palestine after the war. My father said his violin never left his hands throughout the entire journey.

After arriving in Palestine, my father went through a course of basic training at Kibbutz Degania, the first Jewish kibbutz in Eretz Israel, which was founded in 1910. He joined Zionist pioneer A.D. Gordon's team, shared a room with

Return to Zion Like these early Jewish settlers dancing the Horah in Palestine in 1924, young Yaacov Laskier followed his Zionist dreams to Eretz Israel, the Bible's Promised Land, but he contracted both typhus and malaria and was forced to return to Poland to recuperate.

another proponent of Zionism, Joseph Trumpeldor, the renowned Zionist leader who fell in defense of the Tel Hai settlement in 1920, and was among the founders of the Migdal settlement on the shores of the Kinneret, the Sea of Galilee. A few years later, Yaacov contracted typhus and malaria (like many emigrants to Palestine in those days), leaving him dangerously ill.

At the doctor's order, my father returned to Poland in order to recuperate. He was deeply convinced he was not leaving Israel for good, but only in order to return to health. With his departure from Palestine, his first life ended, a period of which he was proud; he would often speak of those days when I was a young girl, with a broad smile and a wistful look on his face.

Yaacov Laskier's second life began upon his return to Poland in the 1920s, when he started his banking business—first in the city of Gdansk (then Danzig) and later back in Bedzin. He married Dvorah (Dorka) Hampel at this time. Their daughter Rutka was born in 1929, followed by son Henius-Joachim in 1937. The Laskiers were a secular, well-established and modern family. In the winter, they went on ski vacations. In the spring they enjoyed excursions in the mountains, and in the summer they vacationed by the sea. The adolescent Rutka studied at the private Furstenberg High School in Bedzin, was a member of a Zionist youth movement and led a very active social life.

Yaacov never let go of the Zionist dream and stayed in touch with Dvorah's parents, who had emigrated to Palestine in the 1920s with some of their children. They settled in Magdiel, a town in central Palestine, and later moved to Tel Aviv. Dvorah Laskier used to send her parents photos of her young children, and that is how some of the family photos were preserved, among them some of Rutka. My father hoped to settle in Israel with his family, but World War II interrupted his plans. It seems that, like so many of those caught up in these turbulent times, he did not anticipate the events the future would bring.

Yaacov's father David Laskier died of typhus in the Bedzin ghetto in 1940 and was buried in the cemetery near the city. In August 1943, a major *Aktion* took place in Bedzin, in which the German authorities passed judgment on the destinies of Bedzin's Jews. [Rutka's notebook includes a description of an earlier *Aktion*, in August 1942.] Yaacov Laskier, his wife Dorka, their children Rutka and Henius and his mother Golda were deported by train to Auschwitz. Rutka, Henius and Dorka were immediately sent to the gas chambers. Yaacov, a strong and healthy man, was sent to labor. He worked for many months, weakening steadily.

One day Yaacov ran into his sister's husband, who told him that the Germans were looking for people whose prewar careers demanded fine motor skills— such as draftsmen and watchmakers—or who had experience dealing with money. My father had been a banker before the war and therefore seemed qualified. Nobody knew what kind of work was involved, or what fate awaited those who left Auschwitz to pursue it, but my father had nothing to lose and so he took the chance. He was transferred to the Sachsenhausen concentration

No. 2/9/2 מס. תרישום	LASKIER	לסקר	בעברית 1 שם המשפחה בשפת ארץ המוצא
	DWOJRA דבורה		בעברית 2 שם פרטי בשפת ארץ המוצא
			3 שם כנוי או שם מושאל
		אברהם	4 שם האב
		גיטל	5 שם האם
		בשואה	6 מצב משפחתי
		1904	7 תאריך הלידה
		בנדין פולין	8 מקום וארץ הלידה
		בנדין	9 השתייך/ה לקהלה/ות
		פולין	10 בארץ
		פולין	11 חגתינות בשנת 1939
		עקרת בית	12 המקצוע

חוק זכרון השואה והגבורה —
י ד ו ש ם
תשי"ג 1953
קובץ בסעיף מס' 2

חפקידו של יד־ושם הוא לאסוף אל המו־
לרח את זכרם של כל אלה מבני העם
היהודי. שנופלו ומסרו את נפשם. ונלחמו
וזרדו באויב הנאצי ובעוזריו והתיצב שם
חבר להם לקהילות, לארגונים ולמוסדות
שהחרבו בגלל השתייכותם עם היהודי;
ולהמרה זו יהא מוסכר —
"...(4) להעניק לבני העם היהודי שנוספו
פדו ונפלו בימי השואה והפרד אורחות־
זכרון של מדינת ישראל לאות האיספף
אל עמם.

	המקום והזמן שנספר		
	אושוויץ 1944		13 המקום והזמן של מותו/ה
	במחנה רכוז		14 נסיבות המוות
	יעקב	הבעל	15 שם האשה
	HAMPEL המפל		16 שם משפחתה לפני הנשואין

שמות הילדים	17	גיל	המקום והזמן שנספר
ר ו ת		14	אושוויץ 1944
י ו א ב י ם		6	" "

18 הכתובת האחרונה הידועה של הנרשם ___ בנדין רח' יאגא 4

19 כתובות ידועות מזמן המלחמה ___ בנדין רח' קורצה 13

אני ___ יעקב לסקר ___ הגר ב ___ ראשון לציון ___ כתובת מלאה רח' לובמן 2
קרוב/ה מלא/ה ___ הבעל ___ של ___ לסקר דבורה
מצהיר/ה בזה כי העדות שמסרתי כאן על פרטיה היא נכונה ואמיתית, לפי מיטב ידיעתי והכרתי.
אני מבקש/ת להעניק לנ"ל אזרחות־זכרון מטעם מדינת ישראל.

מקום ותאריך ___ 6.6.55 ___ ראשון לציון ___ חתימה _____

אזרחות־זכרון הוצנקה	חתימת הפוקד _____
מספר No.	

ה ע ר ו ת מ ש ר ד "י ד ו ש ם"

Documenting the Holocaust This is the Page of Testimony filed with Yad Vashem by Yaacov Laskier in 1955 to bear witness to the deaths of his wife Dvorah, daughter Rutka and son Henius. Yad Vashem now has a total of 2.1 million such sheets, recording the execution of some 3.5 million of the estimated 6 million European Jews who perished in the Holocaust from 1939 to 1945. The document includes a picture of Rutka and Dvorah from 1939, which can be seen larger on p. 15.

camp in Germany, where he was employed in the secret Operation Bernhard. In this Nazi counterfeiting scheme, Jewish prisoners were involved—as artists, painters, graphic designers, engravers and printers—in forging currency, as part of the Nazi regime's plot to undermine Allied economies. They primarily forged British pounds sterling, but also Russian rubles and, toward the end of the war, U.S. dollars.

In the last stages of the war, as Allied troops advanced into the Reich, the members of the Operation Bernhard group, along with their equipment and printing machinery, were sent to the Zement camp outside Ebensee, Austria, for extermination. A group of prisoners, among them Yaacov Laskier, stayed behind at the entrance of the camp. Fortunately, the Allied troops who first arrived to liberate the camp were American, not Russian. The Nazi commander of the camp, as well as the guards and the soldiers, ran away before they could murder all the prisoners. The camp was liberated and that is how Yaacov survived the Holocaust—the only one of his entire family to do so.

Yaacov's third life cycle began when he—a broken man, aware of the loss of his children, wife, mother, brothers and sisters and their families—started to make his way from smoldering Poland to Israel. He stayed for a few months in the Bari displaced-persons camp in Italy, where he worked for the United Nations Relief and Rehabilitation Administration. The ship on which he sailed was caught by the British, who forbade its entrance into Palestine. The refugees were sent to a detention camp in Cyprus, where Yaacov met his future wife, Hannah Wiener, a fellow Polish Jew. Nine months later, Yaacov was sent to the Atlit refugee camp in Mandatory Palestine, where he stayed for a while until he received his entrance visa to settle permanently in Palestine.

In 1947, my father married Hannah, and in 1949, I was born, in Rishon LeZion, a citizen of a new nation: the independent State of Israel. I was named Zahava, after my grandmother Golda (Zahava is Hebrew for Golda), my father's mother, and was the only child of Yaacov and Hannah. Yaacov Laskier—a man whose life embraced three distinct phases, encompassing in full measure the sorrows, the dreams and the heroism of European Jews in the 20th century—passed away in 1986 in Givatayim, outside Tel Aviv. ❖

A New Family Yaacov Laskier poses for a family portrait with daughter Zahava and second wife Hanna Wiener, whom Yaacov met in a refugee camp in Cyprus after the war.

The Victims These are the members of the Laskier family who perished in the Holocaust, as submitted by Yaacov Laskier:

My mother, Golda Zisman-Laskier
Dorka Laskier (Hampel), and my children, Rutka and Joachim
My brother, Yehezkel-Yosef, and his family
My sister, Ester Laskier-Rodel, and her daughter, Lily
My sister Zila, her husband Josef Abramson, and their son, Lipman
My brother Yisrael, his wife Sara (Prawer), and their son, Yehoshua
My sister Gutsha (Gustawa) Laskier-Rottner, and her son, Yosef
My sister Mania, her husband, the lawyer, Yitzhak Zylberszac, and their daughter
My brother Emanuel (Moniek), his wife Bronia (Oppenheim), and their son, David

My Search for Rutka's Family

By Menachem Lior

At the beginning of 2006, I was contacted by Adam Szydlowski, one of the leaders of the Jona Organization in Bedzin, Poland, whose mission is to preserve the Jewish culture of Zaglembie. He told me about the discovery of a diary in Bedzin that once belonged to a young Jewish girl named Rutka Laskier. The diary had been kept by a Polish woman named Stanislawa Sapinska for more than 60 years, according to the wishes of her friend Rutka. In 2006, Sapinska's nephew convinced her that it was time to hand over this now historical document to the Bedzin municipal museum. That same year, the diary was published in its first edition in Poland, edited by Szydlowski and launched with a solemn ceremony. The original diary aroused a great deal of interest—the Auschwitz Museum asked to keep it in its archives—but the mayor of Bedzin decided the diary should be entrusted to Yad Vashem, in Jerusalem.

I was born in Bedzin, and I spent the war years there. In 1939, when the war broke out and the Germans occupied Zaglembie, Jewish schools were closed and Jewish youth movements forbidden. Despite the danger, however, the youth groups continued their activities in private houses, in small groups. My parents' house was used as just such a meeting place, which is how, one day, while boys and girls of the Gordonia youth movement congregated in our house, I met a beautiful girl named Rutka Laskier.

Was this Rutka the writer of the long-lost diary? To find out, I asked Adam about her parents. Adam gave me a few names, among them Yaacov Laskier and Dvorah Hampel, who I knew were the parents of the Rutka Laskier I had met in my parents' home. But I didn't know the fate of the Laskier family during the war. Did any of the family survive? I contacted Linka Gold-Kleinlehrer, a member of the youth movement in Bedzin, who had settled in London, in order to find out if she knew anything about the Laskier family. Linka told me she knew Rutka very well—they were in the same class and Rutka had written a dedication in her autograph book, which she had preserved—and that she believed Rutka's father had survived the Holocaust.

Continuing my search in Israel, I contacted Dalia Mercazi, the daughter of Mordechai Hampel (now deceased) and found out that Dvorah Hampel was the sister of her father. Dvorah Hampel was married to Yaacov Laskier, and they had had two children: a daughter named Rutka and a son named Joachim-Henius. I also learned that Yaacov Laskier had come to Israel after the war, had started a new family and had a daughter called Zahava. I immediately started to look for Zahava, Rutka's sister. With Dalia's help, I found Zahava (Laskier) Scherz. I called her up and told her about the diary.

Adam has given me a copy of the original diary. While reading the text, I was overwhelmed by a strange feeling. I had been given the opportunity to see the children we used to be through the eyes of the adult I am today. We were indeed children according to our age, but we were very grown up, the circumstances of the war having speeded up our adolescence. We were very well informed of what was going on, because after the curfew at sunset, we were in the company of the adults for long periods of time. We listened to their conversations and their evaluations.

I was not a close friend of Rutka's, and of course I did not know that she was writing a diary. However, while reading it, more than 60 years after it had been written and after having read about the events that I too had witnessed, I felt a moment of closeness, of a secret partnership. On March 17, 1943, Rutka mentions a few boys who had "lost their heads" because of her, among them my good friend Moniek. Indeed, Moniek was attracted to Rutka, and he had shared that secret with me. When I read that passage, I knew without any doubt that this was indeed Rutka's writing.

Rutka did not survive and neither did my friend Moniek, but the diary did. In publishing her diary, we are partially fulfilling Rutka's unwritten request to document these events so they will never be forgotten. ❖

Menachem Lior (Lewir) was born in Bedzin in 1928 and was a member of the underground in the Bedzin ghetto. He fled Poland with his parents in 1943, crossed Slovakia, Hungary and Rumania, and reached Palestine in July, 1944, at age 16. He fought in Israel's War of Independence, served a full career in Israel's Air Force, reaching the rank of colonel, and later worked in executive positions in private industry and with the Tel Aviv municipality.

The Holocaust in Bedzin
Bella Gutterman

At the outbreak of the war, some 27,000 Jews lived in the Polish city of Bedzin, making up nearly half the town's population. The Jews of Bedzin called their city "the Jerusalem of Zaglembie." The Jewish community here traced its origins in Zaglembie, Poland's southern cultural and industrial heartland, back to the late Middle Ages. Today, there is no Jewish community in Bedzin. Five years of Nazi occupation, exploitation and murder led to the extermination of almost all the city's Jews.

The Germans occupied Bedzin on September 5, 1939. On the night of September 8–9, abetted by local ethnic Germans and Poles, they burned down the main synagogue while many Jews were praying inside. Dozens of Jewish homes were also burned. The German authorities then published a series of decrees and restrictions, according to which most of the Jews' property was confiscated, and they were forced to pay high taxes, to wear an armband with a blue Star of David (the color changed to a yellow star in September 1941) and to report for forced labor. Zaglembie, including Bedzin, was annexed to the Reich as part of Eastern Upper Silesia, and the city's name was changed to Bendsburg.

In line with Nazi policy throughout occupied Europe, the Jews of Bedzin were made to establish an administrative body headed by Jewish public figures, the Judenrat, which the Germans used as a tool to mobilize forced labor and pillage Jewish property. After a short period, the Jewish community and its Judenrat were subjugated to the authority of the Central Office of the Jewish Councils of Elders of Eastern Upper Silesia, based in nearby Sosnowiec and chaired by Moniek (Moshe) Merin, head of the Judenrat there. The local Judenrat in Bedzin did its best to organize health services, education, housing and, most important, food delivery, but it was soon ordered to concentrate on the transfer of Jews to forced-labor camps.

Dozens of factories and workshops were set up across Zaglembie, an area rich in coal reserves. The Jews of this region were employed by the Schmelt

Sacrilege A German officer poses against the ruins of the Jewish synagogue in Bedzin, which was burned down, as Jews prayed inside, three days after the Germans entered the town. A Roman Catholic priest, Mieczyslaw Zawadzki, whose church stood nearby, saved scores of lives by offering sanctuary to Jews fleeing the inferno.

Organization, established by Reichsführer-SS Heinrich Himmler. Most of the forced labor took place in textile factories, called "shops," which produced clothing, uniforms, shoes, furniture and woodwork. The labor in these workshops was difficult and exhausting, and the wages were meager, but the pay at least increased the workers' chances of buying some food. Whoever worked in a "shop" was also considered vital to the German war effort and thus had a chance of evading deportation to the forced-labor camps operated by the Nazis' Schmelt Organization. The outposts in this chain of some 160 labor

Holocaust scholar Bella Gutterman, Ph.D., is the former Director and Editor-in-Chief of Publications at Yad Vashem. Her numerous works include A Narrow Bridge to Life: Jewish Slave Labor and Survival in the Gross-Rosen Camp System, 1940-45, *published in March 2008 by Berghahn Books.*

Architect of the Holocaust
Heinrich Himmler, one of Adolf Hitler's earliest supporters, was the commander of the SS, Hitler's personal army, which included within it the Gestapo secret police force. It was Himmler who implemented the Nazis' "Final Solution," which sought to exterminate all Jews under German control. Arrested shortly after the war ended, Himmler escaped justice by committing suicide.

camps were notorious among Poland's Jews for their especially bad conditions.

In 1942, pushing to complete the extermination of the Jews quickly, Himmler ordered the concentration of all the Jews in Poland into a limited number of camps. This included the Jewish industrial workers in Zaglembie as well. Himmler rejected requests by German industrialists to retain their forced laborers so that they could continue exploiting them, as well as the attempts by Albert Speer, Germany's Minister of Armaments, to postpone their deportation to Auschwitz so the workers could aid the war effort.

One of the factory owners who asked to keep his Jewish laborers was Alfred Rossner. His textile and cobbler "shops" employed as many as 10,000 Jewish laborers, whom he treated well and protected from deportation. A work permit from Rossner was a better life insurance policy than being a member of the Judenrat. Rossner, a humanitarian, looked out for his Jewish employees, respecting their dignity and even warning them in advance of upcoming German activities. He was arrested for betraying the German cause and executed in 1944. Following the war, Rossner was recognized by Yad Vashem as one of those deemed Righteous Among the Nations: citizens across Europe who worked to save Jews in the Holocaust.

The first deportation from Bedzin to Auschwitz took place on May 12, 1942. It included 1,200 ill and elderly Jews, families with small children and some "unproductive" elements, such as those on social welfare. Another 1,200 were deported in June, and the deportation of most of the Jews from other parts of the region was completed by mid-summer 1942.

On August 12, 1942, a large *Aktion*—the selection of Jews to be deported—took place in Bedzin, headed by Gestapo officer Hans Dreier and the Schmelt Organization representative, Friedrich Kuczynsky. The Jews were assembled for selection in the Hakoah stadium outside Bedzin, the field used by the Jewish soccer team, under the pretext of signing personal documents. This is the *Aktion* Rutka describes in retrospect in the riveting February 6, 1943, entry in her diary. During the *Aktion*, the Jews were divided according to productivity: the working men and the Judenrat members in one group; the women and young people who were to be sent to the Schmelt labor camps, spread all over Silesia, in another. The rest of them—children, the elderly and the unemployed—were sent to their death.

Safe—for Now A group of Jews employed in one of Alfred Rossner's "shops" poses for a group portrait in April 1941. Some 10,000 Jews toiled for Rossner and considered themselves lucky.

At some point, the *Aktion* got out of control, and riots broke out. The mayhem lasted for three long days, during which many Jews were shot on the spot in the assembly area. Polish spectators observed this, as did Germans, including personal guests of Dreier. The Jewish underground movement that was established at the time took advantage of the uproar to save many individual children and even entire families. The *Aktion* in the Hakoah stadium ended with the deportation of some 5,000 Jews to Auschwitz.

By the end of 1942, there was no more doubt among the Jews: they were aware of the fate of the deportees to Auschwitz, as well as of Jews in other parts of Poland and the Reich. The reports they were receiving from Warsaw and Krakow, primarily through Jewish youth movements, left no room for illusions, but they were still hopeful that by working, even in labor camps, they would be saved. At the beginning of 1943, only 61,000 Jews remained in Zaglembie, 18,000 of them in Bedzin. Most of these people were still employed in the workshops.

Rebellion The valiant Warsaw Ghetto Uprising showed that Jews would fight for their lives and altered the Germans' policies toward them in Poland. At right, prisoners are marched from the ghetto. The revolt reached its peak in April and was finally put down on May 16, 1943.

WWII WAR CRIMES RECORDS—NATIONAL ARCHIVES—GETTY IMAGES

Last Stop Jews debark from a train at the Auschwitz station in 1944. Accounts of the mass murders taking place in the Birkenau sector of the camp spread among Poland's Jews in 1943.

In the fall of 1942 the Germans began to concentrate the Jewish population in a ghetto in the Kamionka district on the outskirts of Bedzin. This process continued until spring 1943. It was at this time that the Laskier family was sent to the new ghetto: Rutka's final notebook entry is dated April 24, 1943. Kamionka was a poor and neglected area, overpopulated and unhygienic. Though they were employed, its residents suffered from hunger, anguish and fear of death. The ghetto was not surrounded by fences or walls, but access to it was controlled by guards who enforced a curfew.

At the beginning of 1943, Himmler ordered the factories shut down and the

Schmelt Organization dismantled. In May, the order was given to take apart the workshops and send the Jewish workers to Auschwitz. Historians believe that as a result of the Warsaw Ghetto Uprising, which was raging in April and May, 1943, Himmler decided to sacrifice the high revenues coming from the factories and chose instead to accelerate the extermination of the Jews of Poland.

News of the Warsaw Ghetto Uprising inspired thoughts of resistance in other ghettos, including Bedzin, particularly among members of various Zionist youth movements, such as Hashomer Hatzair, Dror, Gordonia, Hanoar Hatsioni and Bnei Akiva. Two emissaries were sent from Warsaw to Bedzin, the noted resistance fighters Frumka Plotnicka and Zvi Brandes, to head the Jewish Combat Organization of Zaglembie. By the end of 1942, the Jewish resistance movement in the region included more than 200 members.

During this entire period, Dreier continued with the deportation of the Jews of Zaglembie. Some 1,200 Jews were assembled daily at the train station. They were allowed to take money, food and luggage with them. The Jews entered the wagons calmly, aided by members of the Judenrat and the Jewish police of Bedzin. There was no violence. Most of the deportees at this stage were the old and infirm. Despite their awareness of German death camps and gas chambers, nobody wanted to believe that the final destination of these deportees was Auschwitz. Some of them still believed they were going to labor camps.

On August 1, 1943, the final liquidation of the Bedzin ghetto took place, and the Jews were deported to Auschwitz-Birkenau. At that point, many members of the underground movement decided to initiate armed resistance. They quickly dug and hid in bunkers, from which they put up a courageous fight. About 400 young Jews, among them Plotnicka and Baruch Gaftek, commander of the Jewish Combat Organization in Bedzin, fell in battle. During that month alone, more than 30,000 Jews, including Rutka Laskier's family, were deported from the combined Kamionka and Srodula ghettos to Auschwitz.

In February 1944, the last 200 Jews of Bedzin were forced to clean up the ghetto and dig out the bodies of their murdered comrades. Once they had accomplished their mission, they too were sent to their deaths.   ❖

"Something Has Broken in Me"

The Diary of Rutka Laskier and the Writings of Jewish Youth in the Holocaust

By Havi (Ben-Sasson) Dreifuss

Hundreds if not thousands of diaries were written by Jews throughout occupied Europe during World War II, and many of them were lost along with their authors. Among the diaries that survived, those written by Jewish youth are particularly poignant. These were children who matured before their time because of the cruel reality in which they lived, and their diaries can reveal the inner worlds of these young adults, while also illuminating the ways they adapted to the harsh events that took place around them.

Rutka Laskier's diary contains many of the features that characterize the writings of Jewish youth in the Holocaust, especially female children and adolescent girls. One prominent aspect of such works is their illumination of the different circles that make up the adolescent's world. These include the innermost personal circle, the social circle—of major importance to these age groups—the family circle and the general circle. In addition, the writings of Jewish youth in the Holocaust indicate that in these circles, there is a certain duality characteristic of wartime: on the one hand, there are many aspects that typify the life of adolescents as such; while on the other hand, they display facets that are specifically unique to times of war. This tension between normal life and the abnormal reality of the Holocaust that permeates the different circles of adolescents' lives during this harrowing period in history is particularly striking in Rutka's diary entries.

In her writing, Rutka reveals her most personal and innermost feelings, including her own awareness of her emotional and physical development as an adolescent girl discovering her femininity. On numerous occasions her diary provides a kind of echo to her "internal speech," which enables her to address her own self with great openness and directness—writing reminiscent of Anne Frank's addressing her own diary as "Kitty," as well as of the writing of the anonymous boy from Lodz who wrote in four languages in the margins

Dear "Kitty" ... Anne Frank is the best known young Jewish diarist of the Holocaust. The Frank family moved from Frankfurt to Amsterdam in 1933, after Adolf Hitler came to power. Her diary records the two-year period (June 1942-August 1944) during the German occupation of the Netherlands that the family spent hiding in the house of friends before they were betrayed and sent to the Bergen-Belsen concentration camp, where Anne died of typhus at age 15.

of a French book [*see the bibliography that follows this article for information on the memoirs discussed*—Ed.]. For example, on February 5, 1943 Rutka writes to herself, "Well, Rutka, you've probably gone completely crazy," and on March 8 she criticizes herself with the words "What's happening to you, Rutka? You're incapable of controlling yourself."

Like many other Jewish youths, for Rutka her diary is a refuge, somewhere that she can voice her most private thoughts. Thus, for example, she examines her image as if reflected in a mirror, and with impressive directness criticizes certain character traits that she considers unacceptable. At the same time, Rutka is aware of the limitations of writing, and she clearly expresses her frustration over the inability of paper to contain what she is experiencing. On

Havi (Ben-Sasson) Dreifuss, Ph.D., is a Mandel Fellow at the Scholion Interdisciplinary Research Center in Jewish Studies at the Hebrew University of Jerusalem. She wishes to acknowledge the contribution of Adina Drecshler, who shared her thoughts about Rutka's diary.

Next Year in Jerusalem? Young Jews in Poland belonged to a host of youth groups, most of which had Zionist leanings, like these members of the Hatzioni group in Bedzin. Former resident Dasha Rittenberg recalls: "Bedzin was a community of many 'isms'—Zionism, Hassidism, Socialism, Communism."

January 27, 1943, she writes, "I would like to pour out on paper all the turmoil I am feeling inside, but I'm absolutely incapable," and when in her diary entry for February 6, 1943, she reconstructs the terrible August 12, 1942, *Aktion*, she writes, "I can't put it into words."

Rutka's abrupt mood changes are a striking attribute of this innermost circle

80

of the diary. Sometimes, these are caused by the normal circumstances of adolescence, such as unrequited love, low self-image and arguments with friends. At other times, these changes in mood are the upshot of events in the war and atrocities witnessed by the young girl. For example, on March 8 she writes,

> Because of whom or what am I crying? Because of Janek, certainly not.
> Then because of whom? Probably because of freedom. I am sick and tired
> of these gray houses, of the steady fear seen on everybody's faces. This fear
> clutches on to everyone and doesn't let go.

Rutka is also aware of the emotional toll the war is exacting upon her and refers to it explicitly. On February 5, 1943, she writes, "I'm already so 'flooded' with the atrocities of the war that even the worst reports have no effect on me." But Rutka is also aware of another possible reason for this emotional blunting, and the following day she notes, "Something has broken in me. When I walk past a German, everything shrinks in me. I don't know if it is out of fear or hatred."

Beyond Rutka's intense personal circle we encounter her social circle, which occupies such a key place in her writing. Like other youngsters who wrote diaries in ghettos, including her fellow Poles Ruthka Lieblich from Andrychow and Irena Gluck from Krakow, as well as Isaac Rudashevski from Vilnius (Vilna) in Lithuania, her writing reveals the great importance of social life to adolescents, albeit limited by the trials and tribulations of the time. Here, too, one can identify those social aspects that are common to adolescents as such, including friendships with and jealousy of girlfriends; budding love toward young boys; and learning and reading as a social experience. In addition, Rutka's ideological awareness—primarily her Communist leanings—indicates the political consciousness that was so strong among Jewish youngsters in the first half of the 20th century.

For Rutka, as for Masha Rolnilkas from Vilnius, Moshe Flinker from Brussels and Tamara Lazerson-Rostovsky from Kovno, Lithuania, the political realities and their involvement in them occupied an important part of their lives even during the war. But here, too, the Holocaust looms large, whether in the form of Rutka's fear that the changes that would take place in Bedzin would separate her from her friends, or in her description of the streets where girls and boys gathered, as well as "machos" who "undress each girl that passes by with their eyes." The sheer normality of ordinary adolescence that developed not only in the midst of, but above all parallel to, the invasive reality of the war bears impressive witness to the continuation of human and Jewish existence in unbearably bleak conditions.

Compared with her writing about her friends, both male and female, the family circle occupies a relatively minor place in the entries in Rutka's diary. However, we should not overlook the great affection that she expresses for her little brother Henius. Moreover, when she describes how her mother tried to get her to talk in detail about her close male friends, she reveals both her mother's concern for her daughter growing up during wartime and also how she herself viewed her parents. As she puts it, "Lately, I love my parents even more. But sometimes they are so mean to me, it hurts me so much, and then I become hurtful and bad." Relationships between parents and their adolescent children are complicated in the best of times; during wartime, they acquire a further, tragic dimension, as can also be seen in the diaries of Dawid Sierakowiak from Lodz, Dawid Rubinowicz from the village of Krajno near Kielce and Julius Feldman from Krakow.

But Rutka did not concentrate solely on herself, her friends and her family; her diary contains numerous references to the wider world surrounding her. Like other adolescents, she relates to her shrinking space. For example, on January 27 Rutka writes,

> Today I'm in a strange mood. As if I am seized by joy, I am flooded with some kind of happiness I can't explain. As if I was soaked with all the happiness, all the immeasurable distances ... I feel I would have been relieved if I had had the opportunity to stay in a beautiful place, staring at a wonderful landscape. When I'm standing by the riverside and looking at a gushing waterfall, I feel something inside of me being lifted and taken far away.

But a few days later, on February 5, she notes, "The rope around us is getting tighter and tighter. Next month there should already be a ghetto, a real one, surrounded by walls. In the summer it will be unbearable. To sit in a gray,

On the Move—Again Above, further displacement in the Bedzin ghetto. In the Germans' war against the culture of the Jews of Poland, relocation was a commonly used tool. Entire neighborhoods were uprooted, until each family and each person became detached from a sense of community. At right are members of the Jewish Special Order police force, Jews who served as intermediaries for the German authorities and were often reviled.

locked cage, without being able to see fields and flowers ..." On March 1 she describes the crowding that the family had to cope with when they were forced to reduce their apartment to one room, and on April 24, "The summer is already here. It's difficult for me to sit still in the 'shop.' The sun is shining so brightly. Outside the windows, apple trees and lilacs are blooming, and you have to sit in this suffocating and stinking room and sew. The hell with it."

This passage shows how the reality of the threatening war increasingly penetrates Rutka's world. Like other adolescents, she is forced to go out to work

Work—or Die A German officer supervises a labor detail in Bedzin. Workers received meager wages, but as the Nazis adopted the "Final Solution" policy that called for the extermination of the Jews, assignment to a work detail could mean the difference between life and death.

from the early hours of the morning, and in her diary there is an echo of her desire to escape from the world around her by sleeping.

Rutka's diary also demonstrates the extent to which adolescents were exposed to information of the events unfolding around them and how aware they were of the looming catastrophe that awaited them. Like other Poles— Miriam Chaszczewacka from Radomsko, Mary Berg from Warsaw and Halina Nelken from Krakow—both the harsh reality of the ghetto and the rumors from outside it were part of her world. One of the most important entries, which at the same time is one of the most difficult to read, is that of February 6, 1943, when Rutka reconstructs the bloody August 12, 1942, *Aktion* in Bedzin, "So that in a few years, of course if I'm not deported, I'll be able to remember it." After describing in detail the brutal murder of a baby before its mother's eyes, Rutka observes,

> I am writing this as if nothing has happened. As if I were in an army experienced in cruelty. But I'm young, I'm 14, and I haven't seen much in my life, and I'm already so indifferent. Now I am terrified when I see "uniforms." I'm turning into an animal waiting to die. One can lose one's mind thinking about this.

But for Rutka, it was not only the past that held many terrors: so did the future. The day before her description of the *Aktion*, she wrote, "If God existed, He would have certainly not permitted that human beings be thrown alive into furnaces." After a description of the brutal murder of children and old people, she adds—part in hope and part in fear—"[but] it's nothing, as long as there won't be Auschwitz …" Two weeks later, following rumors about what was happening in the towns in the vicinity,

> The town is breathlessly waiting in anticipation, and this anticipation is the worst of all. I wish it would end already! This is torment; this is hell. I try to escape from these thoughts of the next day, but they keep haunting me like nagging flies. If only I could say, it's over, you die only once … But I can't, because despite all these atrocities I want to live and wait for the following day. That means, waiting for Auschwitz or a labor camp.

Some six months later, Rutka's worst fears came true. In August 1943, a year after the *Aktion* that she described so vividly, another *Aktion* took place in Bedzin, and Rutka Laskier and her family were sent to Auschwitz.

Rutka's diary is a quintessential work in the true meaning of the word—some 50 pages, written in a neat, orderly hand, presenting the reader with an entire world. It is a touching human and historical document that reveals the concentric circles that made up the brief life of a Jewish girl. But above all, Rutka's diary reflects the intense inner world of an adolescent girl who in her thoughts was torn between youthful high spirits and the crushing reality of the Holocaust; and in her writing we find an echo not only of her own destruction but also that of the hundreds of thousands of boys and girls whose dreams and nightmares, like Rutka's, were destroyed along with them.   ❖

Adolescent Holocaust Diaries:
A Selected Bibliography
By Havi (Ben-Sasson) Dreifuss

Adelson, Alan, ed. *The Diary of Dawid Sierakowiak: Five Notebooks from the Lodz Ghetto* (New York: Oxford University Press, 1996).

Dawid Sierakowiak of Lodz, Poland, (1924–43) began writing his diary a few months before the outbreak of the war. He describes the occupation of Lodz, the persecution of its Jews and the establishment of the ghetto. In September 1942 Dawid's mother was deported to Chelmno, and in his diary he expresses his deep pain and anguish over her fate. The young diarist died of tuberculosis in the ghetto in August 1943.

Berg, Mary. *The Diary of Mary Berg: Growing Up in the Warsaw Ghetto.* Prepared by Susan Lee Pentlin (Oxford: Oneworld, 2007).

Mary Berg (Wattenberg), born in 1924, lived in Lodz before the war but in September 1939 fled with her parents and sister to Warsaw, where they were confined to the ghetto. Because of her mother's American citizenship, the family was taken for an exchange of foreign nationals with the U.S. a few days before the Jews of Warsaw were deported to Treblinka, and hence they survived. In March 1944, the family arrived in the U.S., and shortly thereafter extracts from Mary's diary were published. But because she described not only the Jews' suffering and distress in her diary but also the social life of those Jews who were better off than others, Mary and her diary, which she had extensively reworked, were the subject of harsh criticism. It is only recently that a new edition of the diary has been issued, containing a description of the events.

Chaszczewacka, Miriam. *A Girl in the Ghetto: A Diary from the Holocaust Period* (Tel Aviv: Radomsko Olim Association, 1978).

In her diary, Miriam Chaszczewacka (1924–42) describes the fate of the Jews of Radomsko, Poland, during the war. On October 7, 1942, Miriam wrote the last lines in her diary as a bloody extermination *Aktion* was carried out in her town. A note attached to the diary indicates that Miriam and her mother hid for a week in a toilet, and when they were no longer able to stand the deprivation and hunger, they gave themselves up to a policeman. The diary has not yet been published in English. (For the original *see* the Yad Vashem Archive, O.3/3382.)

Feldman, Julius. *The Krakow Diary* (Newark: Quill Press, 2002).
The diary of Julius Feldman (1927–43) was discovered in Krakow 20 years after the war, above a lintel, where apparently he had hidden it. The diary describes his experiences during the German occupation of Krakow. After the Krakow Ghetto was liquidated, Julius was sent to Plaszow, where apparently he perished.

Flinker, Moshe. *Young Moshe's Diary: The Spiritual Torment of a Jewish Boy in Nazi Europe* (Jerusalem: Yad Vashem, 1965).
Moshe Flinker (1926–44) and his family were Orthodox Jews who emigrated from Poland to Holland. In 1942, with the growing number of expulsions of Jews from Holland, the family fled to Belgium. In his diary, which was written in an elegant form of Hebrew, Moshe explains his beliefs and hopes and describes his life under occupation—until he was deported to Auschwitz, where he was murdered.

Frank, Anne. *Anne Frank, The Diary of a Young Girl: The Definitive Edition* (New York: Doubleday, 1995).
The diary of Anne Frank (1929–45), a young girl from the Netherlands, has been published in dozens of languages. The millions of copies in print include abridged, complete and annotated versions.

Lazerson-Rostovsky, Tamara. *Tamara's Diary* (Israel: Ghetto Fighters' House and Ha-Kibbutz ha-Me'uhad, 1976).
Tamara Lazerson was born in Kovno, Lithuania, in 1929 into an educated family whose elders attached importance to educating their children in the language of the country. For this reason, Tamara was educated in Lithuanian schools, and she wrote most of her diary in Lithuanian. Tamara escaped from the Kovno Ghetto in 1944 and survived the war. The diary was later published in Hebrew, together with her later memoirs. Extracts from the diary were pub-

lished in English in *The Hidden History of the Kovno Ghetto,* edited by Dennis Klein (Boston: Little, Brown and the United States Holocaust Memorial Museum, 1997).

Lieblich, Ruthka. *A Diary of War* (Brooklyn: Remember, 1993).

Ruthka Lieblich (1926–43) lived in Andrychow, in Silesia, both before and during the war with her parents and her young brother. Her diary covers the period between August 13, 1940, and December 28, 1942. Ruthka and her family were deported to Auschwitz in August 1943 and were murdered there.

Nelken, Halina. *And Yet, I Am Here!* (Amherst: University of Massachusetts Press, 1999).

Halina Nelken was born in Krakow in 1924 to a middle-class family. She began writing her diary before the war and continued it under the German occupation of the city. The diary describes the establishment of the Krakow Ghetto and Jewish life within it. Halina also wrote poems, which were published together with her subsequent recollections in a new version of her diary.

Rolnik, Masha. *I Must Tell* (Jerusalem: Ahiever, 1965).

In her diary Masha Rolnilkas [Rolnik], born in 1927, documented her life in the Vilna Ghetto in Lithuania and in the camps to which she was deported when it was liquidated. Masha survived the war and apparently reworked her diary before it was published in Hebrew and Russian. The book has not been translated into English.

Rudashevski, Isaac. *The Diary of the Vilna Ghetto: June 1941–April 1943* (Tel Aviv: Ghetto Fighters' House, 1973).

In his diary, Isaac Rudashevski (1927–43), a resident of Vilnius [Vilna], Lithuania, documented his life in the ghetto with great sensitivity. When the Vilna Ghetto was liquidated in September 1943, Isaac hid with other members of his family, but two weeks later their hiding place was discovered and its occupants were murdered in the village of Ponary. The only family member who managed to survive was his cousin, and she found the diary when she returned to the family's home after the war.

Rubinowicz, Dawid. *The Diary of Dawid Rubinowicz* (Edinburgh: W. Black-wood, 1981).

Dawid Rubinowicz (1927–42) lived in the Polish village of Krajno before the war. His diary describes the difficulties of living in a Polish village under Nazi occupation. In March 1941, his family was expelled together with other Jews to Bodzentyn, where Dawid continued writing his diary. The diary documents his life until May 1942; a few months later, Dawid and his family were deported to Treblinka.

Zapruder, Alexandra, ed. *Salvaged Pages: Young Writers' Diaries of the Holocaust* (New Haven: Yale University Press, 2002).

At the end of World War II, a resident of Lodz, Avraham Benkel, returned to his city, where in an abandoned house he found a diary written in the margins of a French book, *Les Vrais Riches.* The identity of the boy who wrote his brief record in Hebrew, Yiddish, English and Polish is not known; his fate and that of his 12-year-old sister are also unknown. The diary was donated to Yad Vashem, and an exact replica is on display in the U.S. Holocaust Memorial Museum. (For the original, *see* Yad Vashem Archive, O.33/1032.) A complete English translation has been published in the miscellany of Holocaust writings cited above.

Pankiewicz, Tadeusz. *The Cracow Ghetto Pharmacy* (New York: Holocaust Library, 1985).

Irena Gluck (1925–42) documented her life under Nazi occupation in Krakow and Niepolomice in detail. Her diary begins in May 1940 and ends on her 17th birthday, July 25, 1942, a day when she recorded rumors about a planned expulsion of the Jews of Niepolomice to Wieliczka. The diary, written in Polish, has not yet been published and is in the Jewish Historical Institute in Warsaw (No. 302.270). According to Tadeusz Pankiewicz, the operator of a pharmacy in Krakow and author of the memoir cited above (and honored by Yad Vashem as one of the Righteous Among the Nations), Irena Gluck and her mother were deported to Auschwitz in the October 1942 *Aktion* in the Krakow Ghetto.

RUTKA'S NOTEBOOK

YAD VASHEM

YAD VASHEM, THE HOLOCAUST MARTYRS' AND HEROES' REMEMBRANCE AUTHORITY
Yad Vashem, the Holocaust Martyrs' and Heroes' Remembrance Authority, was established by
the Israeli Parliament in 1953. Located on the Mount of Remembrance in Jerusalem, Yad Vashem
is dedicated to Holocaust remembrance, documentation, research and education. Through the
International School for Holocaust Studies, the Museum Complex, the International Institute for
Holocaust Research and Publications Department, the Library and Archives, the Hall of Names,
and its monuments and memorials, Yad Vashem seeks to meaningfully impart the legacy of the
Shoah for generations to come. Every year, millions of people visit Yad Vashem's 45-acre campus,
and millions more explore various aspects of the Holocaust through Yad Vashem's activities
around the world and online. Drawing on the memories of the past, Yad Vashem aims to strengthen
commitment to Jewish continuity and protect basic human values. *www.yadvashem.org*

YAD VASHEM PUBLICATIONS
DIRECTOR Gabi Hadar **EDITOR-IN-CHIEF** David Silberklang **PHOTO EDITOR** Ayalah Peretz
EDITOR, HEBREW EDITION Adina Drechsler **MANAGING EDITOR, ORIGINAL YAD VASHEM**
ENGLISH EDITION Daniella Zaidman-Mauer **ASSISTANT EDITOR, HEBREW EDITION** Eva Lutkiewicz

TIME

TIME, THE WEEKLY NEWSMAGAZINE
MANAGING EDITOR Richard Stengel
DEPUTY MANAGING EDITORS Priscilla Painton, Michael Elliott, Adi Ignatius

TIME INC. HOME ENTERTAINMENT
EDITOR Kelly Knauer **DESIGNER** Ellen Fanning **PICTURE EDITOR** Patricia Cadley
RESEARCH DIRECTOR Matthew McCann Fenton **COPY EDITOR** Bruce Christopher Carr

The editors wish to acknowledge the contributions of Jeffrey K. Cymbler of New York City,
dedicated archivist of Bedzin's Jewish community.

PUBLISHER Richard Fraiman **GENERAL MANAGER** Steven Sandonato **EXECUTIVE**
DIRECTOR, MARKETING SERVICES Carol Pittard **DIRECTOR, RETAIL & SPECIAL SALES**
Tom Mifsud **DIRECTOR, NEW PRODUCT DEVELOPMENT** Peter Harper **ASSISTANT DIRECTOR,**
BRAND MARKETING Laura Adam **ASSOCIATE COUNSEL** Helen Wan **BOOK PRODUCTION**
MANAGER Suzanne Janso **DESIGN AND PREPRESS MANAGER** Anne-Michelle Gallero **BRAND**
MANAGER Joy Butts **ASSOCIATE BRAND MANAGER** Shelley Rescober

SPECIAL THANKS
Bozena Bannett, Glenn Buonocore, Susan Chodakiewicz, Robert Marasco, Brooke Reger,
Mary Sarro-Waite, Ilene Schreider, Adriana Tierno, Alex Voznesenskiy